T0077891

DARE TO POSSESS-A
GOOD COURAGE!

Steven Barnes

authorHOUSE®

AuthorHouse™
1663 Liberty Drive
Bloomington, IN 47403
www.authorhouse.com
Phone: 833-262-8899

Published by AuthorHouse 06/13/2022

ISBN: 978-1-6655-6117-4 (sc)
ISBN: 978-1-6655-6116-7 (hc)
ISBN: 978-1-6655-6118-1 (e)

Library of Congress Control Number: 2022911255

Print information available on the last page.

Scripture quotations are from the Holy Bible, King James Version
(Authorized Version). First published in 1611. Quoted from the KJV Classic
Reference Bible, Copyright © 1983 by The Zondervan Corporation.

This book is printed on acid-free paper.

CONTENTS

GROW BEYOND YOUR FEELINGS
COURAGE FOR THE PROFESSIONAL

BE STRONG AND OF A GOOD COURAGE
THE CONCLUSION OF THE MATTER

A Dedicated Preface

by Gregory Martin

Would you rather carry around 100 pennies or 4 quarters? Allow me to elaborate. There's an old saying–you are who your friends are. So, I will ask you a follow-up question. Would you prefer four friends of the highest caliber who will cause you to grow as a person and not simply agree with your life choices, but will provide sound feedback if you need a course correction? Or would you prefer to have 100 acquaintances who agree with whatever you say? As I get older, I find myself not having a tremendous desire to make new friends or keep 100 acquaintances. As a matter of fact, I find that I want to cull the herd.

Allow me to introduce one of my quarters. But first, have you ever heard someone say, "That person is like a bad penny?" A bad penny is a person or sometimes a thing that is usually unwelcome, someone or something that appears recurrently, seemingly because fate is taunting you.

In 1979, I was Blessed to meet and begin a 42-year friendship with a fellow United States Air Force Airman. I didn't just get to observe this airman in a professional setting; I got to know him personally during game nights with him and his wife. Boy was he funny! Have you ever been around someone that you find yourself wanting to always be around? That feeling surfaced early.

My friend was not only serving on active duty in the Air Force but working a part time job as a night cleaner at an electric company's headquarters. Wanting to be around "that guy," I convinced him to get me hired as well. Watching this guy work was bewildering! His work ethic was noteworthy. He put his head down and accomplished what should have taken two to three people. After he left, I lasted 30 days! Couldn't do it alone! This airman left Eglin Air Force Base, Florida, for a military base in Belgium. The guy I liked being around left.

In 1988, the Air Force sent me to Moody Air Force Base in Valdosta, Georgia. Shortly thereafter, who do I run across? The bad penny! By then, this guy is no longer an airman but a mid-level sergeant. He had served as an Air Force technical instructor (the Air Force's name for a drill instructor with the Smokey the Bear hat and all). He was even more spit and polish than I had known him at Eglin. Once again, I found myself wanting to be around him. What was it with this dude?

Because of his position at Moody, he had to be the epitome of the noncommissioned officer corps. He was responsible for molding newly appointed sergeants. While serving as the wing executive officer to the base's wing commander, I was responsible for staffing all incoming and outgoing correspondence to the base. So, when the four-star general in command of us sought ONE individual who was above the rest to "on-the-spot" promote under a program named Stripes for Exceptional Performers, who else but the bad penny got the nod. I was so proud to be a part of that. Not only did we grow personally, but the ole drill instructor got to take me to the flightline and teach me how to do a proper adjutant's duck walk for an upcoming change of command ceremony. He does it all!

In 1994, the Air Force assigned me to Spangdahlem Air Base, Germany. The bad penny was stationed in Kaiserslautern, Germany. We would communicate by phone, and I would learn that God had called him to lead a church. He gave me parenting tips. What is it about this guy?

It wasn't long before that bad penny joined me at Spangdahlem. He worked right across the courtyard from me. His military bearing was as tight as ever. He was now preparing mid-level sergeants to be even more effective leaders. He was wiser and more experienced. Still liked being around him.

In 1997, the Air Force sent me to MacDill Air Force Base. I'd have to leave my friend once again. This would be my last duty station before retirement. My friend retired from the Air Force and returned to Valdosta after his Spangdahlem tour, and we would talk on the phone. He was now the full-time pastor of a church. I even had the pleasure of dining with him in Tampa while he was in town to speak at a local church. He was someone people wanted to be around. The charisma never leaves this guy!

Then he told me he was headed to Mississippi to become a civil servant. He was still the friend I wanted to be around! It wasn't long until the bad penny showed up as a civil servant on MacDill Air Force Base—with me again! You know they say God takes care of fools and babies? Well, this fool had been blessed with his friend yet again. This time for keeps. He's put-up roots here. I still want to be around him! His charisma is still there.

For 25 years, I had the tremendous pleasure to serve as a professor for the University of Phoenix. One of my great joys was hiring new professors and preparing them to enter the classroom. After all, I didn't want anyone stepping into the classroom that wasn't going to always give their level best to students. One of the things I'm most proud of is convincing that bad penny to become an instructor. Was I being selfish and coming up with ways to hang around my friend?

I have had the distinct pleasure of being friends with Steven B. Barnes for 42 years. I have stood next to him as his best man. I have had a mentor that (through deeds not words) has shown me how to be your best, always do your best, be dedicated, lead, follow, manage, be a friend, father, and husband. I know a man of faith and have a great example of how to live by faith. I have seen the greatest example of a friend. And you know what, best of all—his heart is bigger than his charisma! Think I will challenge what folks say about bad pennies!

Sincerely,

Gregory Martin, Major (USAF Retired), Former, Professor University of Phoenix and Current, Department of Defense Civil Servant

Photo by Jiatong Tian: www.pexels.com

ACKNOWLEDGEMENTS

(Disclaimer: *I promise this is not a Christian book…
just my story that includes Christianity!*)

My Testimony! First, I owe my everything to the Lord, God Almighty, who is the Creator of everything known and unknown, His Holy Spirit that guides me through every low valley and across every high mountain, and His Son, Jesus Christ, who I believe died for my sinful ways by nature and gives me another opportunity to please The Father through Jesus' sacrifice! I have heard and seen many things in my lifetime, but I am convinced there is a supernatural power and I know Him to be my Saviour, Guide, Keeper, Encourager, Teacher, Shelter, Rock, Hope, Deliverer, and Friend…until the end. Even if God and the Bible were not true, I have become a better human being and man because of my Faith in them. One Friday night in the Summer of 1976, I decided to willfully give my life to God by accepting the belief for myself that Jesus Christ died on the cross, was buried, and rose from the dead and grave, and ascended to Heaven reunited with the Father and intercedes on behalf of all who would accept Him! If not for my belief in the giver and source of life, I would have given up on people, life, and myself early in my lifetime and at woeful disappointing moments in my lifetime; nevertheless, I am yet holding on, all because of Him! John Chapter One declares, "1) In the beginning was the Word, and the Word was with God, and the Word was God. 2) The same was in the beginning with God. 3) All things were made by him; and without him was not anything made that was made. 4) In him was life; and the life was the light of men." This…is when my life began—I am, a Believer! One of my all-time inspirational Gospel songwriter, musician, and singer, the late Reverend Timothy W. said in a song, "Yes, I'm a Believer!"

I must give honor to my earthly mother and father, Mae Frances [Johnson] and Arthur Barnes, Sr., both of Tallahassee, Florida. I am grateful that the aforementioned humans that claimed to produce me through the Divine inception of conception and chose to raise me in fear and discipline in accordance with Proverbs Chapter 23 declaring, "12) Apply thine heart unto instruction, and thine ears to the words of knowledge. 13) Withhold not correction from the child: for if thou *beatest* him with the rod, he shall not die. 14) Thou shalt beat him with the rod, and shalt deliver his soul from hell." I thought they must have recited that Scripture first thing "every" morning and just before bedtime…are there any other Scriptures in the Bible we can study, I wondered… At the end of the day, I am grateful for what may seem harsh and cruel to many but served as a bridge for me to reach Ephesians Chapter 6 mandate, "1) Children, obey your parents in the Lord: for this is right. 2) Honour thy father and mother; which is the first commandment with promise; 3) That it may be well with thee, and thou mayest live long on the earth." Well, I was told that Mae and Arthur are my parents…I accepted that fact of life as well—I am a Believer!

I must recognize my children who in the process of time have taught me far more than I taught them—I am proud of each of them in their own individual way! At 18 years of age, raising my oldest, Shanedra (Nedra), born at Eglin Air Force Base, Fort Walton Beach, Florida was in the words of Frankie Beverly and Maze, joy…and pain—not her fault at all but there was plenty of fast growing up on my part that had to occur. I have always faced *fear* as something that I had to pass through…just as on a roller coaster! Once you are at the peak of the track…the only way off the coaster is to go through the rest of the track. I refer to children as crumb snatchers and life changers! Phase one of my job as parent was done at 40 years of age;

I have learned there are several significant roles and phases of parenthood. Phase one, teach all that you can through their first phase of life through high school; phase two, brace yourself for their decisions that will shape their path and determine your stress; phase three, enjoy the show and the fruit of your labor as they become productive members of society and hopefully grow to be your friend; phase four, pray like you know what that you have done a good job, so they are willing and able to assist you through the final phase of your life and continue the legacy.

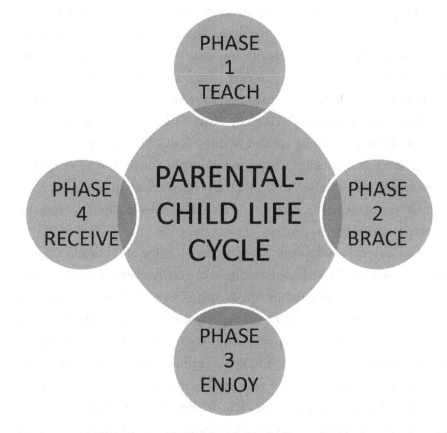

SBB Parental-Child Life Cycle (Steve Barnes)

Then there was Steven, Jr. (BJ), born at Shape Air Base, Mons, Belgium who inspired the ego of manhood in me—popping out a boy! Something must have been in the water, because in just one year and some change,

Stephanie (Step, AKA, Tep-Tep) appeared at the same location as BJ and for quite a while, she was rocking that caboose position in the family. I guess this is the place where I begin the raw and straight-forwardness of this book, I must acknowledge Renee, the loving mother of Nedra, BJ, and Step. Finally, Shelby was born at Moody Air Force Base, Valdosta, Georgia and assumed the caboose position, with reluctance from Stephanie—amazingly, my parenting skills required refinement from 1980 (Nedra) to 1993 (Shelby). I also acknowledge Betty who is the loving mother of Shelby and Dreyton (Drey). There are so many things I could say to Renee and Betty about our relationship over the years, but I will sum it up with a hearty thanks for the beautiful lives we raised together and offer the sincerest apology for all my faults and shortcomings and request sincere forgiveness for any harm to you that I am responsible. In the absence of the parenting book that explained how to raise a child from birth, I relied on what I was taught as explained by Proverbs Chapter 22, "6) Train up a child in the way he should go: and when he is old, he will not depart from it." Additionally, Ephesians Chapter 6 was inspirational, "4) And, ye fathers, provoke not your children to wrath: but bring them up in the nurture and admonition of the Lord." Parenting for me was an institutional process that worked…stick with the process—I am a Believer!

As a daredevil who went beyond the fence line and hooked up with this girl, Regina [Lewis]…what a life changer! According to Sociologist Dr. Morris Massey as cited by The NeuroAlchemist (2016), a Significant Emotional Event (SEE) can be an experience so dramatic that it causes one to consider changing a perspective or value system. When I met the Gal from Guyana—it was an SEE! Regina's unique personality and culture has challenged everything in me, except, my Saviour Jesus Christ! As SEEs occur in people's lives, The Neuroalchemist (2016) mentioned work perspectives could change as well. As a person, I believe I am better because of her…her love for me and others remind me of the love I read about in the Holy Bible! I also acknowledge Regina's parents who accepted me into their family, the late Norris and Janette L., all the brothers and sisters, and her children who have become our children, Keisha, Nicole, Tiffany, and

Marcel. Regina also embraced my children and welcomed my mother into our home—I do not take this lightly.

I will forever be inspired by my younger brother Arthur Barnes, Jr. (deceased, but yet lives) and my little but mighty sister, Tameka "Shorty" Thomas. Although I am the oldest, I have always admired my brother's extreme kindness and my sister's exceptional maturity. I am glad that my brother and I had a chance to grow up together and spent several years together after I retired from the United States Air Force. The way it has worked out, now my sister and I are spending more time together for perhaps the first time since our age gap robbed us of a childhood together. I was shocked when she shared with me that she had no clue who I was as I visited during my leave time from the military. Since I knew her and helped raise her, I always took for granted she knew me but I forgot she was still a toddler when I left for the military. There is another nugget for someone to gleam…take the time to communicate and do not assume. We were taught to serve others and I attribute our Favor of God to a "giving Spirit." My motto for my house: "Living from my Giving, and Giving… just to live!" I must admit, I coined that phrase from a testimony service at church in Belgium, but when I hear things that apply to my life—I hold on, in Faith, for life!

If I acknowledged everyone inspirational to me that would be the entire book! As I write each chapter you will see many others that have been an inspiration to me. I want to conclude acknowledgements with a general list:

- Reverend George W. (deceased); Pastor of Saint Rosa Primitive Baptist Church, Tallahassee, Florida…where I met Jesus! As a child, I knew this man loved God and was in touch…he gained my attention! One of his favorite songs I still remember, "Do You, Know the Man?"
- The Johnson, Barnes, and Dupree Families and all the residents of that 2 mile stretch of Gearhart Road Quarters; my backbone! These are all the people who my parents gave permission to "whoop" my

behind 24/7! Even before surveillance cameras, there was no place to hide!

- Grandchildren, host of relatives, friends, teachers, co-workers, and professional associates; you have given me strength, encouragement, knowledge, and support! I will limit honorable mention to several people who have kept up with me throughout my lifetime and provided mutual support and encouragement to one another with unconditional love...Greg A., Greg Martin, and Sheila W...thank you for caring--enough!

- Chief Master Sergeant Charles P. R. (deceased), United States Air Force (USAF); my professional mentor who steered me straight and saved my military career! I was in trouble up to my eyeballs and he wrote my mom a letter telling her how wonderful of a kid I was...I'm glad he could see beyond where I was standing! I guess... he "spoke things into existence!" I was so honored when later in life I was able to go to his rescue and share some of his impartment into my life back to him in his time of need! His wife was a mom away from home in Belgium and I spent several years with his children.

- Pastor Clifton M., Supreme Headquarters Allied Powers in Europe (SHAPE) Chapel Church of God in Christ, SHAPE AB, Mons, Belgium. What an amazing place to reaffirm my Faith in Christ and start ministry work under this leadership. I sweated out several pairs of shoes!

- The late Pastor R. T. I., Joy Temple Church of God in Christ, San Antonio, Texas; an inspiration to me and a warrior who literally "preached" till death! He taught me consistency and faithfulness!

- Dr. Henry W., Valdosta Deliverance Evangelistic Center, Valdosta, Georgia; my Saul and the one who inspired me to tell everyone despite of what they are going through...to "be encouraged!"

- The United States Air Force...saved my life from the streets and surely incarceration...I am forever grateful! Aim High!

State of Florida Capitol, Tallahassee, Florida.
Source: https://www.loc.gov/

A GLIMPSE OF THE AUTHOR

Steve Barnes, AKA SBB was born and raised in Tallahassee, Florida. He graduated high school 6 months early and despite others telling him he could not, he secured a full-time driver's license clerk position with the State of Florida. He enlisted in the United States Air Force on a military leave of absence from the State of Florida and served 21 years as an information manager, professional military education instructor, postal clerk, drill sergeant, and Commandant. Still, Steve found time to impact every community he was stationed serving in ministry, coaching youth basketball, baseball, and football and a host of Air Force base functions.

Upon retirement, within 2 years, he served as a pastor, managed a radio station, wrote, and edited for a Christian newspaper, lead financial advisor with a Fortune 500 company, Hospice volunteer, and volunteer Chaplain at a major hospital. This was Steve's first experience in society beyond the military as an adult and after struggles with re-entry, he continued with the Department of Defense, United States Air Force General Service employee.

Steve's education includes an Associate's of Science Degree in Instructional Technology and Military Studies, an Associate's of Science Degree in Information Management, a Bachelor of Science Degree in Management, a master's degree in Theological Studies, a Master's of Business Administration Degree with concentration in Human Resources, and a Post Master's Degree in General Business (all but dissertation) with concentration in Organizational Leadership. Steve has extensive training and experience in team building, personal and organizational leadership, business management, public speaking, human resources, human behavior, positive and critical thinking, and education.

He served over 25 years as a professor for the Community College of the Air Force, University of Maryland Europe, University of Phoenix, and the Ultimate Medical Academy. Steve started in ministry in 1983 and pastored for 10 years. Serving in a variety of roles, Steve has counseled and inspired others through major personal and professional challenges for over 40 years. Steve is an entrepreneur and still serving his community and lending a helping hand to others as he is able.

SBB's Preface

This is a motivational, inspirational, instructional, and reality book that I hope provokes thought and action amongst professionals, executives, organizational leaders, family, friends, youth, parents, Believers in God, and non-Believers. I desire to share my Charismatic and realistic story in person that captures my persona in the fullest…Christian, motivational speaker, minister, mentor, listener, Human Resources Manager, military, counselor, financial advisor, life coach, entrepreneur, and teacher all wrapped up into one. Don't worry, my message can be tailored to the audience whether a religious setting or a professional company setting. I tried to emulate the best quality from all those I have served. The bottom-line up front is that after reading this book you can learn from the experiences I have been exposed to and decide to maximize your life…and possess—A "Good" Courage!

By the way…I thought about this book for about 15 years before the serious journey to finally put pen to paper! I was most inspired to write from my thinking spot gazing at Ormond Beach and my office in Apollo Beach! I love the water…

Ormond Beach, Florida. Source: Pexels.com

Apollo Beach, Florida. Source: Pixabay.com

As often as possible, growing up I went to Panama City Beach and now living on the water is the treat of a lifetime! I also use cruises on the water via Ship, boat, and jet ski as therapy to think through challenges I may be experiencing! I've learned instead of lashing out at others…sometimes we just need to take a walk, ride, or just a plain ole nap!

Panama City Beach, Florida. Source: Pexels.com

I grew up playing cards and sometimes my worst hands ended up being a winning hand because I played harder and smarter to maximize the hand. Also, it is key to note that it took a cooperative partner to pull off those wins. The lesson is that we need help coming into this world, living in this world, and leaving this world! The sooner we learn that through humility and non-reliance upon material things, we become better neighbors and friends to one another. Throughout life, I have found myself in a position of serving and helping others and that is the intent of this book. I do not profess to be the smartest man in the room, but I do know my gift in this world and life is to aid and encourage others.

The journey through each chapter of my life is full of wisdom, lessons learned, knowledge, comedy, and yes, other people's stories that I witnessed. I have been planning, meditating on this work for over 15 years, and wanted to write with purpose and not harm any person or institution in the process. On that note, be advised I obtained both informal and formal feedback from editors. Although many names of people and organizations are omitted purposely, the stories and examples are true and from either me or others whom I interacted. At the end of the day, the content is nonfiction and a culmination of my assessment of what it takes for a successful and courageous life.

The more I studied the Bible, the more I saw people and a society that was connected to the events that occurred in the Bible. The connection and approach for this work is my Sunday School class when I was growing up. At the end of the hour, the teacher prepared us for the summary that we had to give of our class to the adults of the congregation. Each student had to explain what he or she learned from the class. In that spirit, I write this book as a summary of the things I have been exposed to generate excitement that results in success for any who will listen and learn…and dare to maximize life! What I learned was from courageous men and women in the bible and it took a *good courage* to stand before the congregation and share the important gems of the lesson. Ultimately, it took courage to tell others that I was glad to accept Jesus as my Saviour, the One, who died for us all! My strange life began that same night as the church folks put me and a few others on the back of a pickup truck about 9:00 p.m. and we rode through Gearhart Road Quarters and stopped at seemingly every house with a light on and all of us who accepted Christ had to tell each homeowner about our experience. I wondered…but obeyed! The lesson was to act upon your Faith immediately before you begin to second guess or worst, lose it!

I discovered a lesson from Bible days that can empower every employee in a company and in turn, cause the company to prosper. In the book of Joshua, out of at least a dozen men sent by Moses to spy a land that was promised to the people of God, Joshua is one of two spies that returned to camp with a positive report! All the spies saw that the land was as promised flowing with milk and honey, but the other spies thought the opposition was too much to conquer, but Joshua and Caleb…Believed the Word of God! Although I did not announce it to the world, I have possessed this attitude or spirit in every position I have held, and naturally, it is optimism, but another way to capture it is…A Good Courage!

Finally, I promise not to overwhelm you with Scriptures in this book because it is not written to one audience. I do hope to have the opportunity to share my experience in person with you, because I know the interaction with one another will inspire us both! Are you ready to widen your perspective on the things you have experienced thus far in life? Are you ready to stop high turnover in your small business? Are you ready to bring your employees together as a close-knit team focused on the goals, objectives, and most of all core values of the organization? Are you ready to stop blaming others for your own decisions? Are you pessimistic but desire to be optimistic? Are you ready to set goals, monitor milestones, and achieve success at a new level? Three, two, one…let's go!

The Bottom-Line Up Front (BLUF)

Possess, A Good Courage

Joshua 1:8-9, "8) This book of the law, shall not depart out of thy mouth; but thou shalt meditate therein day and night, that thou mayest observe to do according to all that is written therein: for then thou shalt make thy way prosperous, and then thou shalt have good success. 9) Have not I commanded thee? **Be strong and of a good courage**; be not afraid, neither be thou dismayed: for the Lord thy God is with thee withersoever thou goest."

Daniel in the Lion's Den. Source: Pixabay.com

Courage does not come easy and to obtain it is a process or system! Merriam-Webster (2020) defines courage as "mental or moral strength to venture, persevere, and withstand danger, fear, or difficulty." May I introduce you to the power of systems and processes? Clearly, this Scripture emphasizes a cause-and-effect relationship. Combining the words of Joshua and Webster, if you obey even in the face of trouble you can expect the building of courage that leads to strength and success! Yes, through focused Faith and assurance that God is with you, your courage can navigate you through challenges towards every goal you set! My goal is to encourage the weary, strengthen the weak minded, and create an atmosphere of motivation that leads you to proclaim, "I can do it!" Yes, you can!

Courage does not come easy, but when you make up your mind to pursue, it becomes easier! I've read the story of Daniel in the Lion's Den and about many other powerful men of God in situations where the odds were against them, but through Faith in God and courage to trust, the outcome was Victorious! Maybe you are not a Bible believer yet…so let's consider John Levitow, United States Air Force Medal of Honor recipient who risked his own life and hurled his bloody and wounded body on a flare in his aircraft and drug it to the rear of the plane to save all on board. Or, I am sure you have seen brave men and women running towards burning vehicles or homes to help others and countless other examples. Courage is that internal instinct that is developed over a period and perhaps you do not realize you have it until the opportunity presents itself. This book inspires you to prepare yourself through hard work and discipline to achieve your goals in life.

One thing that I always instilled in my children was to be conscious of how your achievements in life will help others. You want a college degree, but what will you do with it? Answer the hard questions up front and your courage is on the way! This teaching was inspired through Solomon's writings in Ecclesiastes that to live life foolishly in happiness without purpose is vanity, meaning, nothing left for you in the end! Living with purpose develops courage that is enough for you and others! I dare you to possess a *good courage*!

I know what you are thinking! You do not plan on ending up in a cage with a lion, right? The people I am writing to are afraid to go full force and chase their dreams. I am encouraging you to get off the porch and just start walking towards your goals and aspirations! What is holding you back? Probably like most others fear of failure or the amount of work you perceive. I say you can do it! Just start walking. My company's motto reads, "Speaking things into existence." Just start saying what you will do, and you will soon find yourself doing what it takes to accomplish the task. We spend a lifetime working for some company or business. I dare you to declare yourself a company that chooses to give your services to another company for a period. This my friend will shift your paradigm and cause you to see the world from different lenses. David declared in Psalms 119:105, "Thy word is a lamp unto my feet, and a light unto my path." Just start walking and the spoken word will guide you to victory! I dare you… to possess a good courage! Start walking it with purpose…and speaking it into existence!

Image source: Pixabay.com

Lay a Sure Foundation – Courage for the Parent

CHARACTER IN THE HOUSE

Romaine (2007) wrote a long rant about how uncontrollable some children are and the parents seem to throw their hands up in defeat, but he closed the dialogue with a profound statement—*personal responsibility* for parents to help kids develop positive *character*! This reminds me of a personal emphasis I still continually impress upon my children—make a positive and continual contribution to make the world a better place! Parents are accountable to provide necessities for their child—we get it. Parents are responsible for building character in their child—we struggle! Rather, I am seriously concerned about the common theme in today's society to dress our children in the latest fashion, decorate them in fine jewelry to start the swag, buy them all the latest toys and games, and do whatever it takes to keep them from crying! I will never forget the image of my grandson, Steven III (JB) at about 4 or 5 years old, dressed in the exact same style clothing and jewelry as Steven, Jr. What a hilarious sight...I just couldn't believe what I was seeing, and I just could not stop laughing every time I looked at him in amazement. In the midst of my laughter, I noticed that JB had no expression on his face, nor clue as to why I was so tickled! We watch the news of happenings around the world that includes all the characters and actors that *parents* have created. Somebody has got to accept responsibility, right? In the beginning, babies naturally cry to alert us of one of three essential *needs*: Food, pain, and doo doo on my bootie! In less

1

than one year, some parents train their children to cry for the pleasures of life…perhaps you have seen or heard a display recently. Just like yesterday, I can recall being in a checkout line and there he was at 5 or 6 years old, word for word loud talking mom to get the toy and candy he wanted and refused to put it back. The mom was beyond embarrassment, three shades of red, and felt she had to say something to defend her parenthood in public, so with absolutely no courage nor confidence she raised her voice a little and warned and threatened discipline at the house because of this irrational behavior. Without hesitation, the child responded even louder and more courageously and confidently, "ahhhhhhh mom, you are just saying that because these people are looking!" Literally, I had one arm wrapped around the front of my body holding myself and the other hand was over my mouth! I am sure at a younger age the mom thought those outbursts were cute! Well, I hear that kids now go in time out! In that situation I wanted to call time out for the mom and child abuse and say….SHOCK HIM AND TEAR HIS BUTT UP! Seriously, that is why I would never try that as a child! The time has come that parents must stand up and take their children back! I got it…things have changed; however, guess what? Glad you asked…every time a child is born into this world, he knows nothing, except what parents teach him!

Novak (2018) cited that the Mature/Silents born 1927-1945 got married for life and when they got hired on a job they stayed until retirement as compared to later generations that readily embraced divorce as an acceptable means to an end and frequently job hopped for a variety of reasons. As you can see in my acknowledgements, I am a product of that era and it is my desire to break the curse of divorce in my family for future generations. Listen, listen, listen to me! Many times, we worry about controlling the results and fail to just…do the work! I will expound much more on a day's work later, but for now, just know that nothing is free. Trust the institution that has endured for generations through difficult times and just *do the work*. In other words, teach your children the principles of life and give them a strong character foundation to lean upon in difficult times. Otherwise, you the parent become the rock, and we know that parents cannot be everywhere nor live forever; however, the institution will stand! Trust in the words of Moses in the book of the second law giving, Deuteronomy Chapter 6 "5) And thou shalt love the Lord thy God with all thine heart and with all thy soul, and with all thy might, 6) And these words, which I command thee this day, shall be in thine heart: 7) And thou shalt teach them diligently unto thy children, and shalt talk of them when thou sittest in thine house, and when thou walkest by the way, and when thou liest down, and when thou risest up." Parents, what are you teaching your child? Parents, consider what you want your child to look like in 18 years? Have you considered what you want your child to act like in 18 years? Have you considered what you want your child to talk like in 18 years? It is not too late—stop, look, listen, and act in a manner that prepares your child to face the world…without you, while he still has you!

I am trying to write, but the preacher in me is clawing and scratching to come forth because of the seriousness and urgency of our children, our nation, and ultimately, our world. Yes, I believe we are on a path of self-destruction as written in the Holy Bible how man destroyed himself before. Not convinced of the challenge and still defending your destruction of your child's character by giving him everything you were deprived of during your childhood? I do not have a problem with giving kids nice things, but first, put in the work and precede the gift with responsibility and instructions as Moses commanded. There must be a price to pay if the Nintendo is broken in a month. According to Annie E. Casey Foundation (2018) in 2016 "66% of Black/African American, 52% of American Indian, 42% of Hispanic/Latino" children occupied a single-parent home. This is an alarming statistic because this is nearly 15 million children affected by choices of adults. Please do not take this as a judgment on anyone, but merely a fact to consider as you raise your child now despite the circumstance. My point is to take positive action to truly protect your child from self-destructive ways that have become the norm. Unless parents point out the danger as Sociologist Dr. Morris Massey as cited by Changing Minds (2018) pointed out in his values theory during the "imprint period" ages birth to seven, parents are primarily the unchallenged influence in a child's life and development. Wow! Considering parents have 7 years to teach their children anything in the world and will lose the edge on influence as the child gets older, what is the best use of that time? Seriously, the greatest critic is you—what are you doing with your time?

Romaine (2007) summarized his position with an emphasis on slowing down showering our kids with things, reducing the focus on entertainment, building character through reassurance of their self-worth and life-coping skills. I have a question for you to ponder…how much do you really love your children and what demonstrates that love the most? Think…before you start rattling off things. I see parents who would do anything in the world for their child to like them or behave, but is that the best parents can do for their children? In other words, the parents are catering to the child who has not had life's experiences and learned any better than self-gratification. By nature, humans are selfish, arrogant, deceptive, revengeful, and so many other adjectives that you could help me list. Paul stated in Romans Chapter 3 "23) For all have sinned and come short of the glory of God." Paul continues in Romans Chapter 6 with a question, "1) What shall we say then? Shall we continue in sin, that grace may abound?" Our children are born as a blank disk and parents begin to upload files that will be saved to their hard drives for the duration of their lives. What files are you uploading…the one-eyed monster (TV), You Tube, the latest IPhone, Nike, gold jewelry, rated R movies, etc.? I am not against parents gifting children, but think about when the best time is to introduce some of the things we give them. As a parent, you can manage the heat of peer pressure through ages 5-7 easily as Dr. Massey implies, so do not cave to the pressure from this miniature person bossing you around in the checkout line. I will never forget my 15-year-old daughter (you get three guesses) threatening to call the children welfare people on me during a heated discipline session (use your imagination). At that point, I knew my influence was minimal and I had given her my best as a parent. It appears that when I grew up as a Baby Boomer parents used child psychology on their children when appropriate; in today's society, it appears the children are ruling the Generation Ys and Millennials with parental psychology.

Fast thinking, I could not cave or punk out to this child threatening me, so I told my daughter to go ahead and call the folks—they will pick you up, not me! The response or courageous comeback made her rethink her threat! Parenting is risky business at times, but that got me through that moment—she decided not to call.

This is a good point to describe building character into our children starting at birth filling that empty vessel that is clueless of the world. Romaine (2007) did a great job describing what is on my mind:

"Self-Worth Skills:

- Accepts self with strengths and limitations
- Feels loved and cherished by family and friends
- Has a reality-based sense of competence
- Believes in ability to create meaningful future
- Can sustain loving relationships

Life-Coping Skills:

- Is willing to learn new things
- Can delay self-gratification for the sake of future goals
- Understands and can articulate personal values
- Can identify alternatives and make decisions
- Can appropriately express feelings" (p. 1)

I would like to add my two cents to Romaine's character suggestion. Self-worth skills are extremely important because children need to know they are whole and a valuable part of society. It is not enough for the parent to tell the kid he is important—the kid has to have that inner confidence to know. Remember the 15 million single-parent kids, they oftentimes have a hole in their self-worth because of the things that absent parent would give them. I am sorry ladies and gentlemen, but you cannot be both man and woman! Nature limits our ability to fulfill both roles in a child's life. I cannot tell you the number of young men I have counseled who missed that male fatherly role while growing up. Although these young men appeared fine externally, inside they struggled with the question-- why? The devastating part of that question is no one could answer it for the individual; he had to find his own way to resolve. My role was to help the young men explore the past, recognize reality, and look to the future. If this realization is not resolved, there is a great risk of passing on doubt to the next generation. Ladies, I suggest you stop trying to be Superwoman and recognize your limitations and consider acquiring the assistance of a respectable mature uncle or legitimate organization that provides an example of a man. Men, vice versa—get some help. Stay involved with whatever you decide to do so the child sees your approval and support. Even if not living together, parents should strive to work together so the child has a relationship with both. Children need to experience parental (type) love from both sexes while growing up. Find a way to create some form of a family atmosphere in the child's life so it does not become an "us" against the whole world. The point is establishing a sure foundation that the child can lean on in your absence, temporary or permanent!

Help your child learn who he or she is and allow room for growth and difference from your perspective. In other words, each of my children had different personalities, likes, and dislikes. Unfortunately, I did not fully recognize this point until my last child. A point to note, in my lifetime it seems every decade there is a major change in my perspectives on things, my body, and even the world! My oldest child was born in Generation X and my youngest was born into Generation Y/Millennials—13 years difference. I recall participating in an exercise with several generations and we were asked what we think about money and credit cards. At the time, I was in my 20s. The young teenager's response was as soon as the money touches my hand it is spent and cannot wait to get more. My response had a little more substance because I had a family, but credit cards were golden because they appeared to stretch your paycheck. As the generations continued more wisdom was visible as the commentary progressed to savings, investments, retirement, and ultimately the GI Generation (1901-1926) lived on strictly a cash policy—zero tolerance for credit cards. Time brings change that we cannot control but must find a way to manage. I can see a transition in interaction with my children from no explanation for my demands as a parent in the name of adulthood, to an explanation of my rationale hoping to gain the approval of my youngest. Additionally, I would advise to use caution pushing our children into predetermined careers, etc. I have seen and heard of some successful pushes, as well as disastrous ones full of rebellion and anger. Regardless of your choice, build your child's self-worth.

Tell and show your child genuine love. That does not mean give the child everything he wants, when he wants it, nor bribery for good behavior, etc. As I reflect over my life, I cannot remember my parents telling me they love me nor giving me a hug until I was an adult! I am not angry about that because they showed love in their own learned way. My parents came from large, hardworking families and I'm sure if you got a meal…you felt loved! For that reason, I focused on telling my kids I loved them and hugged often as a greeting, for challenging moments, and for victories! Prioritize teaching your children the basics in childhood and preparing them for that entry point of peer pressure. Build that foundation and instill it in them. For example, some parents teach their child to pray, memorize in case of emergency phone numbers, how to handle a stranger that approaches him, etc. Finally, allow your child to see you demonstrate what you teach to the best of your ability and situation. Make sure your child knows you, your family, and the world needs him. Start discussing the future and allow your child to explore interests—do not worry if it is not what you want… children change their minds…just like adults!

Romaine (2007) equally noted the necessity of life-coping skills. I feel parents have an easier time building the self-worth presence in their children but seem to struggle with the life-coping skills. Why? My theory is that our own growing up experience can affect what we do or refuse to do, and this can negatively affect our children. As humans we seem to struggle with our behavior and self-discipline. We do not like rules! We do not like change! We do not like being told, no! One of my greatest lessons in life is learning how to accept what I considered negative feedback. The feedback was only negative because I did not want to hear it. However, soon I learned the value of listening to those things I did not want to hear. My ground rules were that I needed to know that the person providing me the feedback cared about me as a person and wanted to see me mature and develop. How many people practice handling challenging news with their kids? Remember Dr. Massey's imprint years and teach this critical life-coping skill. As a child my lesson on attitude was simple, but the argument is still debated whether it worked on me. Raise your hand if you grew up *back in the day* and you enjoyed getting beatings from your parents. Just what I thought—no one! Right, so when I got a whooping, I got mad and wanted to do something about it, but I felt helpless and afraid simultaneously. I can recall going in a corner, licking my wounds, and pouting! Well, after the wild man from Sudan (Dad) got me again for pouting, I soon learned that I had to find another strategy. That was the lesson...did not take any discussion. I got it! Now I am faced with the challenge to teach my children how to cope during anger and challenging news. By the way, while stationed in Brussels, Belgium in the 80s I crossed paths with a church member that continually testified she had "no complaints, just thanks!" Then across the sanctuary someone else proclaimed, "no more bad days... just challenging moments!" I now make a concerted effort to remove the word *bad* from my vocabulary and that automatically puts a more positive outlook on whatever state I find myself. Herein is the lesson shared by Apostle Paul in Philippians Chapter 4, "11) Not that I speak in respect of want: for I have learned, in whatsoever state I am, therewith to be content. 12) I know both how to be abased, and I know how to abound: everywhere and in all things, I am instructed both to be full and to be hungry, both to abound and to suffer need. 13) I can do all things through Christ, which strengtheneth me." Well, go ahead and shout, AMEN! Our kids need to know how to deal with both good and challenging circumstances before they happen! Our children need to know how to be rich and how to be in need. There is no need to get overly excited or unnecessarily saddened. Yes, and in sports...winning and losing are critical lessons to learn for the good of the institution.

When college players could celebrate touchdowns in the end zone, I can recall a football coach that taught his star player a valuable lesson with many implications. The coach said, "Son, when you score a touchdown, act like you have been in the end zone before!" Now as a parent, we wear many hats and one of those primary hats during the imprint period is *leader*! Perhaps the leader in you can do a better job than the mother or father in passing along the life-coping skills your child needs. One more thing before I explain, I find another persona that interferes with this valuable lesson of life-coping skills is parents desiring to be more of a friend than a mother or father. Friendship needs to grow over the years and has no place during those early years of a child's life. Why does this occur? I suspect that there could potentially be some voids in the parent's life and the attempt is to fill those voids, although the parent may not consciously realize what he or she is doing. Therefore, I recommend parents schedule personal time away from the child and give your child some leisure time away from you. This is healthy and actually a part of teaching those life-coping skills. In the article Inspiring Behavior (2018), the leader is encouraged to remove his emotions, as well as the individual's emotions from conversations that involve a desired change in behavior that is perceived as negative. Further, the article suggests before engaging in the conversation to understand the individual's core values, clearly state the reason for the conversation, stay focused on one point, most importantly, give the individual an opportunity to express how he or she feels about the *objective* (no emotions) information you just presented. In reflection, remember if the coach or leader is talking to his or her child, the core values are well known because you are the originator! Clearly stating the reason for the lesson is easier said than done for a parent! However, the leader and coach in you want to teach a lesson for life and the parent in you is mad...right now! I can recall expressing to many women that would scream and yell at boys for several minutes straight in anger and frustration and feel a sense of accomplishment. However, boys soon learn that all I have to do is hear, not listen to the noise and then proceed to what they want to do with no change—just hope mom does not catch them doing it again. However, if you want a boy's attention, associate consequences with the infraction and a conversation can take place. I have taught college level students for over 25 years and whether it is speaking or writing, when it is time to communicate you should state the objective up front! This tells listeners what you are about to say. Beating around the bush can destroy your message before it begins. If you approach your child in anger, you are temporarily insane and really are incapable of a rational conversation. At the end, you nor your child will remember half of what you said. I learned to study…to be quiet! I learned that sticks and stones may break my bones and words can hurt me also! For example, on Gerhart Road, pick a house and there was some whooping going on daily! I can recall a discussion where a person's father beat him down the old-fashioned way on a regular basis. Later in life after the child was about 40 years old, the father and child remanence, and surprisingly the father has no recollection of the discipline sessions. Wow! Really? Remember, I am a critical thinker, so I pondered…why? As I objectively analyzed why, I thought about the generation of the father that was full of anger, racial tensions, and so much more! I continued thinking and thought about the parents of the father and what he may have been exposed to visually and physically. In that generation was something known as slavery where guess what happened? Yes…brutal beatings. Objectively, like it or not, I can reason within my mind how beatings can be forgotten. Remember the power of courage to carry you through impossible situations. The mind is super intelligent!

Cool down, get yourself together, narrow your anger to one main thought, and schedule a time when you are ready to talk. This cool off period is good for you and the child. You will discover the conversation is shorter, more effective, and longer lasting. Once you have communicated your point, it is a good time to allow for a response from your child. I know what the Baby Boomers are thinking…what? Yes, times have changed…not the standard! It is time for a new approach for new crumb snatchers. Like it or not, society will not tolerate beatings of old.

I discussed less with my older children and reasoned more with my youngest for a variety of reasons. The techniques were different, in the end, I feel both strategies were effective. Although I may have discussed challenges with my child, at the end of the day, I was the parent and would make the final decision. When I grew up there was great emphasis on home training. The theory was as the child would behave in public as he was trained at home.

Childhood is a very delicate time in a person's life because the parameters are set that guide decisions to a certain extent...for life. Oftentimes, we judge the product of childhood, but to a significant extent, I have concluded that parents own much of the responsibility. For example, I recall attending a workshop for health wellness and discussions occurred at each table. A young lady in her mid-30s at my table shared the most interesting concept I had ever heard. As we discussed healthy food choices, the lady exclaimed that her children did not eat candy, nor did they like candy. At this point, I was all ears, eyes, and mind to hear more about what I thought was impossible up to that point in my life...about 39 years old. The lady explained that she never introduced her children to candy and sweets during their early years and instead cut fruits and vegetables in fun shapes, bagged them, and gave them to the children for snacks. Therefore, by the time the children tasted candy it was not pleasant.

By nature, I am an analyzer and critical thinker...so I began to ponder this lady's wisdom and how I could use the theory although my kids were already beyond their early years. I began to reflect on the things I was introduced to and wondered...what if!

As I was residing at a timeshare for a week and working on my book, I met a retired Navy Chief, and we had a very stimulating conversation about our experiences and plans. What a healthy exchange—uplifting, encouraging, and mutual sharing! In any case, as we discussed our travels to places within Europe, he mentioned one spot we both visited in Malaga, Spain and how his 14-year-old boy was exposed to topless women on the beaches. I am sure the boy's eyes were wide open and his expression revealed his pleasure! I made a point to the Chief that is an example of what we have to be responsible for when there are challenges that arise later—as a parent, we have to know that we had a role in the behavior of the child. I do not bring this up as good or bad, but just things parents are responsible for with kids. While I am on the topic, I might as well share my experience in Germany at the swim bad (swimming pool). As a newcomer, I thought I would take a nice family outing to the swim bad and take advantage of a nice summer day in Germany. As we were spreading our blanket and claiming our spot, a German lady about 15 yards away from us undressed totally at poolside and put on her bathing suit. Forget about the kids…I was in shock and acting like a dumb American staring with my mouth open! I was just totally caught off guard. However, after that day at the pool, we had to decide about the kids—should we go back? The decision was made to frequent a different pool.

My brother and I like guns and use to enjoy hunting small game. Why? Because dad took us hunting with him frequently and we were the vine shakers and got to finish off an animal with our BB or pellet gun to minimize suffering. We eventually graduated to the same 12-gauge shotgun dad used to hunt. There were no child locks in the house; we were trained when it was appropriate to handle the gun. There were many days and nights my brother and I were home alone, but we never considered playing with the guns. My brother was a Lieutenant for the Leon County Sherriff's Department, I joined the military, and we both obtained a firearm carry permit. I never thought about it, but dad was an influence on the desire to own a weapon. Now that the idea about influence is clear, what would happen if parents carefully planned the precious years of their children from birth until at least 7 years of age?

Sociologist Dr. Morris Massey, as cited by Changing Minds (2018) explained that people are not born with values but develop them during three periods: Imprint (parental influence), up to age 7; Modeling (copying others), 8-13; Socialization (peer influence), 13-21. I am sure with the technological advancement and Generation Y and Millennials the timeline above has shifted to the left because of the ease of social media and access to television and the Internet. Many have nicknamed the television as the one-eyed demon referring to the material young children are exposed to at a premature age. Seriously, it started in my era as I recall one of my younger cousins walking around as we played holding his crouch at about 5 years of age exclaiming, he wanted some pussycat. As kids we laughed at this little snotty-nosed kid, but from a parental perspective, this was reckless behavior. Now this same young man is in prison for life! My point is the greatest time of influence for parents is the early years as the young lady I mentioned earlier taught her kids to embrace vegetables and fruit, she actually extended their lives. What if I had started eating healthier, earlier? Because of my poor eating habits, I struggle with medical challenges that could have possibly been avoided or minimized. I mention this not to blame anyone, but to make the point of how critical decisions face parents who obviously love their children. Now what…will you do? When your child is ready to leave the nest and start interacting with teachers, television, healthcare members, coaches, etc. they will begin to mimic things they do and speak. A far worst threat is Massey's socialization period when kids challenge parental rules because what their peers think is more important. If I had known then, what I know now I would have made some changes. Trust the institution, stay the course, chart a new path when necessary, and be of a good courage!

The first memorable character builder I can recall is ***an honest day's work***! I still cannot believe it, but my mom filled a notebook size sheet of paper with "a list" of 15-20 chores Monday through Saturday when I was home. Any hope of pleasure was preceded by work! Work preceded school homework—that is how serious my work ethic was embedded. Back in the day, kids in America were stuck to the television for cartoons on Saturday morning. Guess what? Yes, I had to get up early and complete "the list" before I could watch cartoons. According to Marketing Teacher (2018) the Baby Boomers were the first television generation. I was 4 years older than my brother and because he was ill quite often, and I was 15 years old when my sister was born, I did all the chores for boys and girls to include learning to cook. My ticket to homework or playing outside with my friends was "the list!" As a kid, this just did not seem right to work so hard, but I soon mastered a technique to get it done in minimum time. In my house, completing the tasks too fast meant they were half done, so I had to put some serious thought into announcing that I was finished. I appreciate the lesson that nothing is free!

Because of "the list," I became an entrepreneur in my neighborhood and at school. After the bills, clothing, and lunch money for school, there was no such thing as an allowance. I had to find a way to earn money legally, because I was taught stealing was wrong. At school, I sold candy, hot cinnamon toothpicks, comic books, and traded "goods." Sometimes I might share personally classified information and unless there is value added for the point in the story, some things are simply better left not spoken. In my neighborhood, I cut grass and raked leaves. As far back as I can remember, my dad had a few jobs to make the ends meet. One of the jobs involved delivering packages on a truck like FedEx or UPS and I would ride with him, run the packages up to the porch, and earned a few bucks. My maternal grandfather was a farmer and plumber, and I would ride with him during the summer and weekends on his jobs and assist him with the plumbing and raked leaves and straw from the yards of his customers. I can recall my grandfather's request for help one day at his house. This was an all-day job so I was sure this would be a big payday. At the end of the day, I kept waiting around for my pay before I rode my bike back home. After it was obvious granddad was not going to say anything, I asked him for my pay. Granddad's reply was, "Boy, didn't you eat lunch today?" I almost cried as I exclaimed that he promised to pay me—until he reached in his pocket and gave me a shiny dime! Then I cried! There was another childhood lesson, it is not always about money. The next day I was ready to go on our next job together. Somehow, I always managed to have money to spend and money saved. Why?

At some point in life I adopted the motto: Living from my giving, and giving, just to live! If I stop giving, I stop living and vice versa. As I reflect on my childhood years, giving and sharing is what I noticed. When the corn was ready, a hog was slaughtered, and the watermelon was ripe, everybody got some—neighbors, friends, and family. This was my life as a kid and my family did not give what they did not want, but they gave what they would eat or use. Furthermore, the late Horace G., my father-in-law,

Renee's dad gave me a lesson for life when he explained to me how he was able to grow sweet cane every year—replant the best cane for the next year's crop. Now I can analyze this notion of a Mature/Silent (eat good cane for life) as compared to Generation Y/Millennium (eat good cane today) and understand conversations with others. Even in discussions I find the need to give allowance for people who may not understand me so that we might find a compromising point. For example, I can recall while working at the American Embassy in Brussels, Belgium, Nedra was in daycare and the director wanted to speak with me because she observed Nedra spanking her doll. I shall never forget the splendor and eloquence this over educated childcare director explained to me Nedra's problem using her psychology educational background. What I remember from that conversation I still use today…she exclaimed that to connect with my daughter I have to enter into her world of understanding and communicate at that level as opposed to what I would say to an adult. Wow! What a Blessing in my life! This is what I give to others to help our conversation—understanding! I offer a challenge to adjust your conversation to those you are communicating with and I know you will notice a better response in return. Well, when it was my turn to talk to the director, at a boastful 19 years of age, I gave her the Tallahassee translation of what Nedra was doing—spanking her doll the same way she got spanked! I wish I could copy and paste that lady's face into this book right here!

As you can see, living, giving, and working were all intertwined together…for the good of everyone! Romans Chapter 8 reminds us that "28) And we know that all things work together for good to them that love God, to them who are called according to his purpose." Work was not random, but with much purpose! Keeping your mind on the purpose of the work made the work easier to finish.

Where there was a desire to do something fun, there was a prerequisite for work. For example, when the state fair came to town it was pecan season and that was the ticket to get that extra cash—pick and sell pecan. I was amazed at what happened year after year on my 4-mile neighborhood road. Just about everything required to live was grown or raised…hogs, cattle, corn, cane, peas, beans, watermelon, the list goes on. Everyone helped each other and shared—get the concept…work then reward. Shall I add teamwork? I learned so much on those early mornings and late evenings. The hog killing was fascinating to me and I wanted to be there from the time the man loaded the rifle to shoot the hog that had been selected long before that day and then another man would quickly cut his throat. Nothing was thrown away as each person knew what to do in this annual event during the winter. Galatians Chapter 6 encourages us "9) And let us not be weary in well doing: for in due season we shall reap if we faint not. 10) As we have therefore opportunity, let us do good unto all men, especially unto them who are of the household of faith." I have learned to just keep giving, just keep living, and just keep working and due season will come again and again to the point there is no lack. We must give our kids something as parents and I gave my best according to what I knew would get them to the finish line. Lacking a how to raise a kid instruction book, I used the knowledge that I acquired through experience.

According to Marketing Teacher (2018) my kids crossed two generations—Generation X (Nedra) and the rest were Generation Y/ Millennium. Fortunately, we were able to provide them opportunities and gifts (nurturing), but Baby Boomers raised them. Everybody had a chore to earn an allowance that increased with age. As the money was given, so was a lesson on money management. As Hempfield (2016) explained, the 10-10-80 rule was in full force and you will never be broke—10% to God, 10% to savings, and live on the 80%. As we grow older, this should just be the starting point, but we can increase the first two numbers and decrease the latter. Remember, I am a Believer, and I tell you when you stick to the principle, you get more back than you give. The bottom line on work is found in 2 Thessalonians Chapter 3 "10) For even when we were with you, this we commanded you, that if any would not work, neither should he eat." My kids learned the value of work and now as they are seasoned adults in their late 20s and 30s they are working, but not aimlessly, but chasing their dreams and goals. I must admit it is rewarding to see the ultimate plan come together. I learned home training was critical to public behavior! I can recall visiting my parents' friends and the kids played together while the grown and sexy folks talked! Kids were not allowed to hang around adult conversation and to look in one's mouth was surely a beat down request. After arriving at these friends' home, never failed they would have the best treat you can imagine as a kid…fresh cake or cookies, etc. Before we left home, we were drilled not to ask for anything or accept anything because it would give the appearance we were not fed properly at home! OMG! What torture that was as a kid. Just imagine for a minute placing a bucket of KFC chicken in the middle of a floor and telling a dog to "sit" and not eat the freshly fried chicken. The friends literally had to beg my parents for us to get the food because our mouths were quietly and reluctantly saying, "no Ma'am," but our eyes and body language said otherwise. Yes, when visiting I ensured my kids had the appropriate meal of the day, but if offered a treat they were allowed. The takeaway is the values were instilled in me for what needed to occur within the home, but a little more practicality was allowing the child to accept, but not ask. Practice makes perfect!

VALUES AND DISCIPLINES
GAINED IN SUNDAY SCHOOL

Even if you do not believe in God, the Father of Abraham, Isaac, and Jacob, sharing the Christian story about Jesus Christ will help your children become better citizens. Deuteronomy 6:5-7 has saved my life and provided a guide for each generation of my family: "And thou shalt love the Lord thy God with all thine heart, and with all thy soul, and with all thy might, 6) And these words, which I command thee this day, shall be in thine heart: 7) And thou shalt teach them diligently unto thy children, and shalt talk of them when thou sittest in thine house, and when thou walkest by the way, and when thou liest down, and when thou risest up."

I recall my earliest experience with learning the respect of a higher being was reciting grace before a meal, "God is great, and God is good, let us thank Him, for this food! Amen!" This basic model has changed and expanded over the years, but it was here that I learned to be thankful for things many lack! Through these prayers of Faith, I learned the value of ensuring my kids had food at each meal and oh boy did Mom get creative when food was low in that last week of the month. Oh yes, sometimes we had breakfast food for dinner, but she made sure we had the essentials and a piece of meat with every meal. I could tell you some stories, but the frequency of some of those meals is why I no longer can stomach spam, chicken hot dogs, sardines, nor Vienna sausages! My wife suggested some fried spam for dinner one night…that one got heated and no, I did not eat.

Another spin off Sunday School was learning the Lord's Prayer each night before going to bed. Again, a model of an extended and situational prayer that I now pray that encourages me to think about others who may not be as fortunate. I can recall some scary nights for several reasons, i.e., will Dad wake me up when he get home to whoop me for what I did that day, a big football game the next day, or the courage to ask that girl to be mine! I learned how to work those prayers for the good. However, it was these innocent prayers that instilled in me the need to look to a higher being in times of trouble as an adult. I can recall countless stories of Prisoners of War who attribute their survival to remain hopeful to God, prayer, or the American Flag. This writing is about strengthening your courage and one sure way to do this is to learn to pray…in Faith believing the possibility of obtaining what you need. I must admit…I feel much stronger when I am praying for a need in comparison to a want.

In the Gearhart Road stretch, also known as Johnson Quarters (my Mother's maiden name), Deacon Cunningham would drive his pickup truck and pick all my playmates up for Sunday School which was about a 6-mile drive. In all those years, I cannot recall one incident where someone got hurt as we were packed in and some sitting on the side of the truck. Of course, with the discipline of today's youth there would probably be an accident each trip of some sort. Sunday School lessons worked hand in hand with the basic values of home and school. I cannot emphasize enough the value of instilling respectable long-term manners in children while they are young and curious about life. It saddens me to see children encouraged to do things for a laugh that will surely be a problem in school and on a job. In my head, this three-pillar child teaching model made me the man I am.

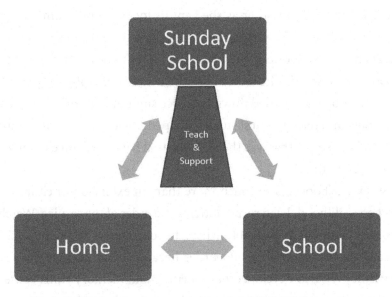

3-Pillar Child Teaching Support Model (CTSM) (Steve Barnes)

I can recall speaking with a co-worker who emphatically stated that she would never take her children to church so that they would have a choice whether to serve God! I thought to myself wow…how would they have a choice if they were never exposed? I can recall straying away from the appropriate behavior I was taught, but there was never a time I could escape the values I was taught in the three-pillar illustration. Those values were etched in my brain and supported one another in so many ways. Sometimes I could hear the Sunday School teacher's voice, at other times I would wonder what my parents would think if they could see me in action, and of course, I could imagine the disappointment from my favorite teachers. OMG…voices in my head! The 3-pillar CTSM model is exactly what I used to lead and guide my kids even now.

My Godmother, Ms. Elvenia H. formed a "Sunshine Band" that was essentially an extension of Sunday School. We had yellow tops and dark bottoms and we met monthly on Saturdays and learned how to conduct meetings, plan and set goals, and built another sense of community. She enticed us to always come because after the meetings she had the best food. We planned fun outings and community service and looking back I can see the worth of Godmother as she kept us focused on becoming a good citizen. I shall never forget the time we got in a little trouble as we visited a rural church. One of our members was always known to skirt the line of trouble and why did he look under the bench at the boy in front of us? OMG! The boy was dressed down in a nice suit but had some roughed-up work boots and once the first snicker slipped, the entire row of our group just could not stop…that was the last time that happened once Godmother got finished with us!

Sunday School was so much more than an extension of church. As I reflect on childhood, I can recall noticing the order of the service. Watching the order of things is probably where I took interest in business. I still basically do things in a certain order because I can predict the results every time. We also developed our listening and memory skills as we had to share with the class at large what we learned each Sunday. Again, public speaking was in the making and now I desire to be a motivational speaker. It is my hope that my story opens doors for me to inspire others ranging from the classroom setting to corporate America…the story is the same and so are the results! There was a reward system in place, such as, snacks, fruit, and candy. What an inexpensive price for lessons that would drive life. As a child I would have skipped Sunday School, but I am so glad that my parents made me attend; once I knew I did not have a choice, I started enjoying the experience and looked at the positives.

In case you are wondering, yes, my children went to Sunday School to learn all the things I experienced. Proverbs 22:6 declares, "Train up a child in the way he should go: and when he is old, he will not depart from it." I can assure you that those words are true. Once I graduated high school and joined the Air Force, I thought I was home free from Sunday School and church! Once in basic training going to chapel was a way to escape the drill sergeant on Sundays so I went. I even made it to my first assignment and again…no interest, I thought I had escaped! While stationed in Brussels, Belgium, I met a young Black man in the Army, David L. that locked into me and just would not leave me alone. He was a reminder of all the things I had learned about the Bible and he just got on my last nerve every time I saw him. Eventually, I surrendered, rededicated my life to God and returned to church driving about one hour each Sunday to the chapel on Supreme Headquarters Allied Powers in Europe, Air Base. These memories and my experiences are simply supernatural! Pastor Clifton M. was a great encouragement and became a friend that I touch base with every so often. Under Pastor Melvin's leadership, I acknowledged the call to preach the Gospel everywhere I go, and this is just another opportunity in this writing!

Sunday School also gained me recognition with my professional mentor for life—Chief Master Sergeant Charlie P. R., who was from Montgomery, Alabama. My first base was at Eglin Air Force Base, Florida in Fort Walton Beach; from there, I was assigned to Brussels, Belgium in the Air Postal Squadron located at the Brussels Airport Mail Terminal. Chief Charlie had the grueling task of leading a group of young Airmen to manage incoming and outgoing mail for the American Forces in Brussels and throughout Europe and even Africa. Chief as we called him was the most unlikely person to become my mentor as he was a short White male Caucasian, chain smoker, and looked like what I would call a Red Neck! Yet, he took interest in me and was another person God had in place to remind me of parental guidance and Sunday School values and discipline. Chief became a father figure to all of us while in Belgium and bailed us out of trouble repeatedly with love and concern. He called everyone "Sarge!" For anyone else it would be disrespectful, but I observed Chief call Colonels and dignitaries, "Sarge." I got in enough trouble to be harshly disciplined and Chief wrote my mom and told her how good of a child she raised and how proud he was of me. That really blew my mind after my mom told me she received his letter…by the way, she still has it 37 years later and wants me to frame it! LOL When Chief retired, he had a 2-3-inch-thick file of bad stuff on me and gave it to me before the new Chief arrived! Ladies and Gentlemen, that move scared me straight and was a part of my not departing from what I was taught as Solomon exclaimed in Provers 22. Between Chief Charlie, David, and Pastor Clifton, I did not stand a chance at escaping God!

Back to my children, yes, they tried the same escape plan, and you would know God had a plan for them as well. Listen, the pay back is you raise kids that are not dependent upon the parent but rely on prayer to God! What a Blessing it has been that I heard my Mom and Dad share with friends that their kids never nagged them weekly for assistance. The joy to my ears to hear #3 child say, "Dad, I was in a situation and did not know what to do, but I decided to call on Jesus...!" Oh my was I shouting for joy! The best gift that I ever received...I continue to give him away... Jesus Christ as my Lord and Saviour! My Faith has delivered me through many situations and provided so many opportunities. The older my kids get the more I see the same driving qualities of business, love, giving, hard work, endurance, Faith in God, and success! Yes again, their kids also know who God is and His importance in their lives. Remember Deuteronomy? Every generation must know for the legacy to continue. Parents be of Good Courage and teach your children so they will have a fighting chance after you are gone! As I move on, let us sing the Sunday School song: "Sunday School is marching on! SUN-DAY, SCH-double-O-L, Sunday School is marching on!"

This is my 3rd location I am writing from…
one week at the Tuscany Village Resort.

Orlando Florida Landmarks. Source: Loc.gov

DISCIPLINE AT SCHOOL

Released from the House – Courage for the Child

WHERE BOYS BECOME MEN...THE UNITED STATES ARMED FORCES

G rowing up the buzz was the "Vietnam War!" My two Grandmothers stayed two rocks' throw away from each other and I can recall them sitting in a rocking chair in front of the television praying for God to bring their sons back home. I had uncles on both sides of my family in the war. One of my favorite Aunties, Kaye whom I hung out with almost every day of the Summer was married to a Vietnam Vet, David. Thinking back... perhaps I was her therapy to cope? He came home and brought photos of some of the action and I was in total shock to see photos of what was **not** on the news. After a U.S. soldier was killed, the enemy would do terrible things to the body and the U.S. soldiers would return the favor. The stories of what the U.S. leadership would do to boost the morale of the soldiers so they would keep fighting was also interesting and shocking to me. Little did I know these stories and experiences with my Aunt and Uncle would be the foundation for my own military career. As a kid, I never dreamed of joining the forces and if anything, I was not interested due to the image of war. The other value in this time with my Aunt and Uncle is my brother and I spent time in their home on the weekends and that too was therapy from our own home where we experienced traumatic stress from family challenges, as do others. In one community, there was a lake in the middle along with a shared canoe for residents to use because there was a store on the other side. One day, our canoe flipped and without hesitation, I had to literally save my Aunt who swam worse than a huge rock! I attribute my natural skills to my Dad who had me in sports, boy scouts, swimming, auto repair, landscaping and track and field—primarily running from him when I was in trouble! In any case, with no lifeguard experience, I simply repeated what I saw the lifeguards do at the pool when they had to pull someone out and amazingly, it worked. It was a challenge, but I managed to get her to lay back into my chest with one arm underneath her neck to secure her and I used my right hand and feet to tread the water slowly until we reached the bank. I am not sure you ever tried saving a drowning person, but it could be a dangerous experience for both as the drowning person fight the water while simultaneously attacking the swimmer. In a nutshell, that is how the military and sports work…train, train, train and when the situation occurs you do not think, you just naturally react to what you were trained. I have learned to master the benefit of processes and systems…the way everything in this world operates. There may come a time to change the process but know that the process and system is where protection lies. As we witnessed Americans attack on our nation's capital in January 2021, I knew that the Republican nor Democratic Party could support such an act because of the strength of processes and the system in place. No regard to politics or party affiliation, the controlling American way of life cannot be challenged in such a manner by force or much more than the cause would be a risk.

Speaking of the system, after my parents divorced, I thought I was the man of the house, but my Mom saw things a little differently. I made the false assumption that because I was working two jobs, had my own car, and was helping with household bills that I was an adult ready for the world. Well, one night me and somebody fell asleep and the next thing I knew… it was sunrise! My emotions went from scared to death to a false sense of confidence that Mom could not do anything about it. However, I was not so confident about my girlfriend's Dad…I felt like I died twice in one sunset! The girlfriend's Dad worked overnight fortunately, and he was not home yet. I got her home and I know her Mom did not buy the story we sold, but she warned I had better get out of her house before Papa Bear arrived if I was enjoying life…I expeditiously took that advice and I do believe I passed him on the highway!

Upon arriving home, Mom was impatiently waiting and strongly encouraged me to join the Army! I called her bluff and spoke with the Air Force recruiter that same week on my day off! Additionally, President Jimmy Carter was discussing the possibility of another draft and I translated that as Army! Based on my childhood experiences with Vietnam, I wanted no parts of that type of duty; rather, I figured if I was not a pilot that my experience should be more civil. I completed my high school credits in December and was just waiting around for graduation in June. The recruiter found me an opening in September, but I just hate having something to do staring at me! After a couple of weeks, I went back to the recruiter and requested the first Greyhound Bus to San Antonio! My date quickly changed to July and I was excited about this new challenge. Mom cried as I left, but I did not understand why since it was her advice I was following.

Upon arrival at the San Antonio Airport, I knew at that point…I was on my own for the first time and my first few steps a short dude came up to a group of us and started barking out instructions. I thought I had made a huge mistake, but that decision to join the Air Force has turned out to be one of the most successful decisions I have ever made! Raised in the South in a strict family, I got in more trouble for laughing than anything else during basic training. I saw others crying because they could not make up their bed, fold their clothes, or many other basic tasks. My family (system/process) had prepared me well for this experience… perhaps I was verbally abused at basic training, but I had already been both verbally and physically abused (by today's standards) as a child. My Drill Instructor eventually started calling me "Smiley!" I even managed to get him to smile in a few serious moments when he should have been serious. I shall never forget my first Air Force Mentor, Staff Sergeant (SSgt) Larry C. ask me why I remember his name without trying. People who impact us in a positive manner are etched in our brain computer for life! Recall I discussed values are locked in early in life as a child, I believe that process starts all over again at probably two other occasions—adulthood and senior citizen status. As a child, parents are the greatest influence on those values of right and wrong. As a young adult…all my peers caused me to challenge the rights and wrongs of my parents although they were etched in my brain computer. Again, The Word exclaims in Proverbs 22:6, "Train up a child in the we he should go and when he is old, he will not depart from it." Good, bad, and ugly, I have found this statement to be true!

At 17, the Air Force maximized that exploration of values as I was away from home for the first time with no restraints! Yes, the training wheels were off BABY!!! Now there were two of me struggling for power in my daily and long-term decisions. Although I was in the same body, sometimes people were talking to "Stevie" and other times my new persona…"Steve." Stevie was no match for this sprouting thoroughbred quarter horse! For example, in basic training SSgt Cross soon realized Stevie was a solid Airman with discipline, knowledge, and experience in following instructions and leading others and selected Stevie as a squad leader. Stevie had his squad tight…they could march in cadence, make tight beds where quarters bounced, produce inspection ready wall lockers and masterpiece clothing drawers with all the contents folded at exactly 6 inches. However, Steve felt overlooked and wanted some action! One weekend, Steve sucker punched Stevie and joined a 45-man pillow fight! Well, when Monday came Steve got Stevie fired and once again…it was funny. On one occasion during open ranks inspection while standing at attention (no movement allowed), after SSgt Cross had went to a rear rank, Steve being up front saw a female formation marching by and he took the liberty to look and turned his head as they passed. All was well until Steve returned his head back forward and about 6 inches from his nose was the Squadron Commander who immediately pulled Steve out of the formation for counseling. Somehow…there was no smiling that day with the threat of being pushed back in training. Again, the emphasis is on the Process and System (P & S) of discipline! Discipline is two-fold! The old saying goes when it comes to discipline that we spend 80% of our time with 20% of the people that do not conform. When leaders do not discipline, it serves as an invitation to others to also violate rules but worse, it is a demotivator for those who do conform.

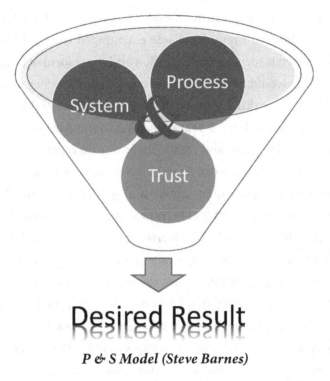

P & S Model (Steve Barnes)

Steve had to realize quickly that Stevie's character would lead to survival to successfully complete Air Force Basic Training. Interestingly, this was the first glimpse of Steven! We talk about split and multiple personalities... like an alcoholic, at least I can admit mine! The P & S that Stevie valued early in life focused him on the end time where a good and reasonable lifestyle and choices will lead to a peaceful and ripe old age. First, that you would probably live a full and productive life, and secondly, that you would mature and grow through that middle peer driven Steve guy! Steven oftentimes reminisces on the arrogant Steve, but longs for the values of the cooperative Stevie. The question is who are your personas that you mask from the world but support and defend throughout multiple work, play, and family challenges? What process do you have in place that values your future? Steven was focused on the benefit of the decision that Stevie's foundational character led Steve to make in joining the U.S. Air Force. The struggle is real, but the P & S for me was ensuring Stevie and Steven were strong enough to ultimately defeat Steve! Stevie was taught at school, home, and Sunday School to share, Steve was encouraged to eat, drink, and be merry, and Steven is focused on succession and some form of legacy for the generations that would follow him. Obviously, as soon as Steven's existence surfaced, decision making improved and life was more stable. Stevie and Steven were committed to a 4-year obligation to the Air Force.

Graduation Day came and went…there was no one there to celebrate the third greatest success story in my life—accepting Jesus Christ as my Saviour, graduation from high school, and graduation from the United States Air Force! Somehow, I had become somewhat a loner as I separated from my childhood friends and started high school and beyond. The decision to be a loner was not intentional or unintentional, it just happened as I struggled to deal with unpleasant things that I was exposed to during my childhood. I am positive that I was not the only person to experience abuse, violence, and sexual behavior all at an age too early. As I counseled an employee as late as 2021, she also expressed similar experiences that drove her to isolation, shame, and silence. I was writing this very chapter during that conversation and was able to share the P & S Model that would surely bring her through the pain. The pains I have experienced in youth have resulted in gains I shared in adulthood. Trust the process and system! In 1979 after graduation from basic training, I was ordered to remain at Lackland Air Force Base (AFB), Texas because my technical training was scheduled at Keesler AFB, Mississippi where a hurricane was forecast. Steve showed back up and was not having it for Airmen that were scheduled to be discharged boss him around all day doing landscaping chores each day… seriously? Stevie showed up the first day to get his rake and assignment for the day. The second day, Steve showed up, got his rake and filled his day with enjoyment and a schedule of his own. This continued for approximately 2 weeks until he was transferred to Keesler. Upon completion of technical training Steve was stationed at Eglin AFB, Florida where he met a friend for life, Greg Martin. Steve and Greg bonded naturally and spent many hours and days together, were stationed at the same base a couple of times, and without planning both settled in the Greater Tampa, Florida area after retiring from the Air Force.

Becoming a man started quickly at age 17 with marriage and one year later hello Shanedra! Speaking of process, I could spend the entirety of this book sharing my amazement of the birth process. I recall being proud and scared but even though I did not have a clue, I found that the P & S Model was enough to figure things out. Money was tight and I found myself spending half of the grocery bill in one aisle for the smallest person in the house. Once again, Stevie and Steven saved the day and strong armed Steve to take a seat…"Baby on Board!" Realistically, I literally had to sacrifice numerous things I desired for the care of my family. I can recall cooking a different flavor of Hamburger Helper each day of the week and other thrifty meals to make the dollar stretch. Amongst several negative things I witnessed as a child were far more positive things that prepared me for that moment of husband and father. The courage of my parents had prepared me for the ultimate responsibility of raising a child. I did not like chores, discipline, going to Sunday School, changing my baby sister's diaper, nor putting forth the work it took to make good grades, but these are the things that prepared me to nourish and teach a child of my own. The process and system worked! After only one and a half years at Eglin, my family was transferred to Brussels, Belgium. I had never heard of Belgium and had to go to the library to research this foreign country. I was a one flight veteran boasting my only trip to San Antonio from Tallahassee. I then found myself preparing for a 6-hour flight over the Atlantic Ocean to a strange place and people. I stood on the same courage that I used as a kid to stand up as a shy boy and accept Christ, the same courage it took to stand up to a bully, Charles in middle school and refused to give up my lunch money, the same courage to join the U.S. Air Force, and the same courage it took to accept my ultimate responsibility as a father. The beauty with courage is it builds just like faith…***courage does what faith believes and causes fear to surrender***!

One of my greatest financial mistakes was purchasing a brand new 1979 Pontiac Grand Prix! My excuse was my car kept breaking down, but I found out in the end it was a $2 part—gas filter! My Father-in-law encouraged me to spend $2,000 or so and paint my car and do whatever to feel better about it but I did not listen. I even shipped the new car to Belgium and indeed it was a bragging piece, but I simply could not afford the car and ended up selling it to a co-worker. That financial spiral did not stop until 10 years later when I sat down with a financial advisor who illustrated to me, I had $600 unaccounted for each month. I knew the money came in, but I did not know where it went. In Belgium, I must admit I got in enough financial trouble to be in serious trouble with the Air Force, but God introduced me to my mentor, Chief Charlie P. R. who showed me compassion and started me on the road to recovery. Courage takes time to develop and the more intentional the faster the development. Stand up to the bully…whatever it or he! I always thought one had to be rich to invest, but consistent investment and savings over time is the key! Chief Rogers was the most unlikely person in my mind to be my mentor. He was a White male from Montgomery, Alabama and I frankly did not trust him. However, we spent hours on the autobahn delivering mail to multiple countries. I do not know why he always picked me to go with him! Chief taught me to always greet others, ask them how they are doing and wait for an answer, and let them know when I needed help. I watched Chief get us out of numerous bad situations by using the technique he taught me. On one occasion we ran out of gas with no money or credit card in the middle of France and I was about to panic at 19 years of age. Chief pulled up to the pump and said, "Sarge, fill it up!" I teach those under my leadership to obey now and challenge later, so I filled up the tank. I watched Chief convince a total stranger to let us go without paying for the gas and to send the bill to the U.S. Embassy in Paris which was our destination. I watched Chief obtain enough sports equipment for me to start a community basketball and softball league in Brussels, Belgium. In Brussels we were responsible for the mail delivery to the Americans and transferred other mail to numerous other countries. Chief created the motto: "We dose, but never close!" I kept up with Chief until his transition to Glory! I was a reckless fool as a young man, but courage made me a better man for family and the world!

I have spent my entire life under strict scrutiny…from strict parents in Tallahassee, to Uncle Sam, aka, the military, to Department of Defense Civilian, to now Amazon partnership. Collectively, each of these entities taught me life survival skills, provided protection, disciplined me to respect standards, and literally built my "good courage" that ultimately made my life worth living! I have apologized to my kids as I continue to grow older wisdom continues to teach. However, there is a line from the movie Back to the Future that said, "If you change one thing, you change everything!" Therefore, it is what it is, and I cannot change the past, but I can affect the now that will affect the future! The Bible encourages us to not worry about tomorrow and it took me a minute to understand that thought fully! We often talk about leaving a legacy for others and the way to do it is "now!" Got it? We cannot do the future because the future is a result of the now… which one day will be the past. Ah I am troubling your mind a bit to generate thoughtful energy that will stir up that good courage in you.

Stationed in Brussels there was no U.S. military base, but we serviced the U.S. Embassy, North Atlantic Treaty Organization (NATO), NATO Support Activity and a host of other surrounding countries and that extended great opportunity to learn the culture and locals. I consider Europe as my second home since I lived there a total of 16 years. I found much of the culture was like growing up in Tallahassee! Chief told me to return to Lackland AFB and become a Military Training Instructor (MTI)—a Drill Sergeant! My fear and inadequacies said, "no way!" However, knowing Chief had wisdom and had shared so much insight with me about life, people, and the Air Force I trusted his words and took good courage to apply for the unknown! I got accepted and I could not believe that I was selected as the top graduate from the largest class in history at that time! I have never held a more rewarding job working one on one with 50 recruits at a time and molding them from civilians to Airmen in 6-week rotations. After two years of working with the enlisted, I was selected to work with officer candidates for two years. I must mention

Technical Sergeant Robert "Bob" S. was a key mentor during my time as an MTI. I tracked down my own now Master Sergeant Larry C. and was expecting him to say how proud he was of me returning to give back and he only had three words for me, "You are crazy!" Chief told me as an MTI I would gain extensive counseling skills as many of the recruits connected to me and chose to speak with me instead of a Chaplain on many occasions. As time drew near for another assignment rotation, I enjoyed teaching and applied to teach in the classroom and got accepted at Moody AFB, Georgia as a Professional Military Education (PME) Instructor. There I was literally teaching my peers which was both a challenge and Blessing as they also had much to share with me. There I ran into my friend Greg from my first base. We both had matured in our own ways and before our relationship was kids play, but now we helped each other professionally. At Moody, the Gulf War started, and I found out that if I were not in the special duty PME assignment, I was #1 on the list to go and serve. I will never forget the feeling on that night the air campaign started, as I was preparing to play a squadron basketball game, I felt the camaraderie of my fellow Airmen that left from Moody…I wanted to be there with them! I originally joined the Air Force for a number of reasons, but it was not solely patriotic. My good courage challenged me to get hired by the Florida Department of Highway Safety and Motor Vehicles at 17 years old as a state employee. I do not like it when someone says that I cannot do something. However, I have matured to disallow people's challenges, but rather, overcome my own fears and pursue good courage! Representative John Lewis was known for "good trouble," but I want to promote good courage that is also…life changing! I found that doing what people challenged me to do shortchanged my personal goals and gave me an easy way out to avoid "good courage." The state of Florida gave me two 4-year leave of absences to test out the military, but when the mommy's bluff turned into Gulf War patriotism, my commitment and attitude to the military changed…I became a career Airman! In a positive way, what people wanted me to do was no longer the priority. This is the point I sat down with the financial advisor and started planning for my 20-year retirement and I wanted the option to leave and start another career. Remember the "lamp unto my feet and light to my path" earlier? Well, you do not need all the answers before you start walking…just start walking and the answers will reveal themselves when you need them. Imagine walking through the house of mirrors at the fair. I have heard stories where people spent half their day trying to get through it and others literally walk right through with minimal false turns. The point is just start in good courage and "look" for the answers you need…they may come from a child, from an event, from a news story, or from a conversation with a friend. I will also share with you that your answers will not look like you imagine, and the source will be unexpected. Just keep walking and keep looking and most of all, keep speaking things into existence to selected people.

After completing four consecutive special duty tours away from my primary Information Management job in the Air Force, I received orders to Sembach Air Base (AB), Germany. Shelby was just born at the Moody hospital and that was a fun experience that led to a challenge of taking a newborn to Germany in the cold winter. After 2 years in my primary position, I was accepted to teach PME again at the Noncommissioned Officer Academy and did some more growing up! Again, working with my peers but at a more senior grade we exchanged so many wonderful experiences to challenge one another to developing good courage! When I became an MTI, I began to realize that I had so much to give others to help through difficult situations, but I also realized in helping others I was also helping myself. In other words, how could I help them overcome their fears without dealing with my own? There is the lesson, giving to others is a perfect way to grow your courage—purpose! Our main characters in this book are Joshua and Caleb who saw giants in a land they were to possess just like the other spies! Joshua and Caleb looked beyond their own limited capabilities to a higher source of psychological power and took good courage to believe the giants could be overtaken. You too, can defeat giants in your life through good courage. I propose that many of your giants are as the Wizard of Oz…puny bullies that hinder your dreams. The challenge is to stand up to the bullies and fight one time and then continue your good courage journey to your destiny. Say it now…"Yes I can!"

I finished my career in the military, in uniform, at Spangdahlem AB, Germany as the Commandant of another PME school and what another position to have direct influence in the lives and careers of others. After much effort to apply for the position and get selected, that small voice of doubt always tries to resurface. This reminds me of a man who would take dogs to a small town each weekend to fight each other and he would take bets on which dog would win. No matter who won or lost, the man would always win and make lucrative money. Someone wondered how the man always knew which dog would win. The answer was simple, all week long the man would feed one dog and malnourish the other—he bet on the strong one! The lesson is you must feed your courage to make it strong and not malnourished! Food for courage? I would define some good courage food as education, experience, growth, mentors, and hanging around three types of people: 1) Mentors…those who inspire you; 2) Peers…two-way positive encouragement; 3) Others…who are sincere and need your help. While we are parked on this thought, let me also mention the three types of people I discovered in the book of Nehemiah when he was instructed to rebuild the wall: 1) Producers; 2) Consumers; 3) Complainers! Exercise, exercise, exercise! This is the term we used in the military to practice for war! Declare your life a war zone now and defeat is unacceptable—take good courage now! The exercise is for you to examine the people in your life right now whether friends or relatives. Who are they? Spend your time with those who sincerely need your help and who sincerely want to be helped! I often run across people who know they need help but cannot be quiet long enough to listen and continue to provide "an excuse/defense" for every suggestion to start building their good courage! Are you that person?

After retiring from the military, I had to figure out what was next for my life. I thought I knew but maybe it was a forced "logical" decision that was more of what I could see (works) as opposed to what I could not see (Faith/good courage). Wow…after retiring I was Pastoring, Christian newspaper writer/editor, hospital Chaplain, financial advisor/team leader, and radio station manager and morning show host. This brings up another interjection, do not be afraid to try new things in your plight to your ultimate dream or place in society. Do not be surprised or afraid when bizarre opportunities come your way to navigate you along the path to where you belong. According to Workopolis (2018), your generation could affect how often you change jobs and careers. For example, younger generations are more likely to change than older generations. Futurist Rohit Talwar as cited in Workopolis (2018) stated today's generation of children can expect to work as many as 40 different jobs in 10 different career paths. As I examine my own experience, I have held 35+ positions in 10+ industries and finally arrived at what I feel is my purpose in life! Guess what…it is still happening as I am embarking on maturing the good courage for the author, personal and professional coach, and motivational speaker breaking out. I did not plan for that to happen…I just kept walking and had to step up to the challenge and take good courage believing my "now" actions prepared me for "future" opportunities. Therefore, when the opportunity presented itself, the exercise, exercise, exercise had prepared me. Some call this process rebranding, resetting, or starting over; I see it as a driving, continuing, and evolving process.

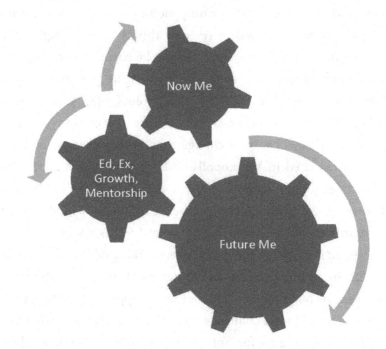

Education, Experience, Growth, & Mentorship Gear (Drive) Model

The book of Ecclesiastes 9:11 reads, "…under the sun, that the race is not to the swift, nor the battle to the strong, neither yet bread to the wise, nor yet riches to men of understanding, nor yet favour to men of skill; but time and chance happeneth to them all." I can see this Scripture in the model and in my life as I reflect on my past. We are running a marathon and not a sprint, so get a pace that you can maintain. I will also share with you a Blessing I discovered while at a low point in my life—three "Ps!" I believe God spoke to me and encouraged me to look for **progress** and not **perfection** and I could always see **positive** happenings. Reflection has driven me all the way back to my earliest childhood years! I consider myself to have become an entrepreneur (Future Me), but I can recall running candy, comic book, sports cards, and many more businesses as a grade school kid supplementing my lunch money I was given. The money was not enough to fulfill my perceived needs so instead of begging and complaining I was self-taught how to become a "producer" and not a "consumer." What else influenced me you might wonder? I watched adult family and friends around me work hard every day outside of punching a formal time clock. I helped my dad on his part-time jobs of package delivery and office cleaning. I helped my grandad with plumbing and I also worked on the plumbing customers' yard in between doing tasks for grandad. Another huge reflection point is I played Monopoly at least a couple of times a week for many of my childhood years and even with my children as they were old enough. Time and chance happeneth to us all…but you must enter the race and declare yourself a contestant for your dreams! When I ran those packages from my dad's Tallahassee Moving and Storage delivery van to the doorsteps, I never had a clue that I would be partnering with Amazon delivering Prime packages to the doorsteps of customers. When opportunities present themselves…you cannot get ready, you must be ready. If the opportunity "happeneth" to you, know that your "good courage" is strong enough because of the education, experience, growth, and mentorship drive in your life.

I found that every 10 years a major shift occurs in our surroundings whether it be society, family, or even our own lives. As I reflect one decade at a time, I see major changes in my life and way of thinking. Why? It is the "happeneth" that has occurred that influences my good courage. Therefore, as much as possible, I want to make sure I have some positive "happeneth" going on in my gears in the illustration above. After retiring from the military, I flew through several jobs simultaneously for 2 years trying to figure out what I was supposed to be as an adult! Remember, I skipped normal, civilian adulthood! I joined the military at 17 years old and basically grew up inside that protected institution and was subject to the Constitution of the United States of America and the more restrictive Uniform Code of Military Justice. Commercial break…so it really bothers me I must admit seeing Americans who refuse to serve in the military irresponsibly declare their rights without understanding the price paid for those rights throughout the American history. Back to live…here is another "happeneth" to me. One day I was supposed to meet a group of gentlemen to discuss an upcoming concert and we agreed to a time. Of course, I arrived early and waited, and waited, and waited for almost an hour past the agreed upon time. When the gentlemen arrived, I inquired as to what was the hold up? They arrived within a few minutes of each other. One of the gentlemen explained, "this is how we roll." About one or two months before this happened, I had decided to apply for a government position back in the Department of Defense as a civilian employee. I had received a job offer for a job that I did not want in a place where I did not want to live. Shortly after this experience with the men, I received a call and email asking me if I still wanted the position that I had basically ignored for months. I realized the transition from military to civilian was a culture shock. Understand, the typical job offer expires after 3 days in the federal system. This "happeneth" to me was a sure sign that I should accept this position and I did despite of my preferences. Through the process of time and several job changes, I went from Georgia, to Mississippi, to Tampa, to Apollo Beach where I currently reside doing what I was destined to do... leader, teacher, human resources, and entrepreneur. The reason you cannot tell everyone your dream is because they are not in the group of people, I mentioned earlier that you should keep in your inner circle. I have learned that many people around you do not mind seeing you do well...just not better than them. Looking back on the "happeneth" to me from the time I left high school till now, the boy has become a boy-man and is transitioning into a boy-man-senior (Stevie, Steve, and Steven). I hope you hear what I am saying? The opportunity to learn, gain experience, and grow never ends...in this life! I summarized my plight in life in thirds: 1) Military; 2) Civilian-Military; 3) Civilian. I am drawing near the end of the second phase and already planning for the third, to maximize the days which are precious and few.

THE SOURCE...OF INSPIRATION...GOD

Do not be offended or disturbed by acknowledgement of who I believe has kept me, is inspiring me, and will secure me...that's God who is the author and finisher of my Faith and Courage! I find that everybody has somebody or something that inspires them to do what they do! I just choose a specific God and not just the generic term. By now you know I am a Christian who believe the Holy Bible is true with all my heart, mind, body, and soul! Guess what, if none of it is true, believing it is has made me a far better person and contributing member of society. I can tell you with that if it were not for the love of God in my heart, only a very few people could tolerate my persona!

Hear my story and TEST-imony! I first heard about Jesus Christ, God, and the Holy Spirit when I was forced to go to Sunday School as a kid. It started out as Jesus is love, etc. This is also when my Godmother started the sunshine band for the kids in my community and she further instilled Godly principles in me. My first sincere interest in deciding to become a Christian by my own confession is when I saw Reverend George W. preach so hard on Sunday that he could not really turn it off when the Spirit was moving upon him. I was further inspired as a kid when I learned that he could not read but would deliver powerful sermons in service that I must admit were piercing my heart because of his conviction and anointing. I soon began to seek Christ as my personal Saviour and did in the Summer of 1976, the year my baby sister Tameka was born. I shall never forget the night my grandfather prayed towards the end of the revival and I confessed Christ that same night and the Deacons and Mothers started at one end of Gearhart Road stopping at each house where I had to share my Faith for about 2-3 miles. I could not believe that was happening. Next, I remember getting baptized in Lake Jackson early one morning and that water was cold! Of course, as soon as I was out of mom's house, I could not block God out of my mind, but I did not practice my faith. Earlier, I shared the Scripture with you that if the child is taught…he will not depart! When I reached a low in Brussels, I turned back to God 100 and even drove to church one hour, one way, rain, shine, or snow! Pastor Clifton Melvin was also instrumental in leading me to the ministry at Supreme Headquarters Allied Powers in Europe (SHAPE) Chapel. From there I went to San Antonio, Texas under the leadership of Pastor Reuben T. I., Joy Temple Church where I was ordained as an Elder. I then transferred to Valdosta, Georgia under the leadership of Dr. Henry E. W., Evangel Temple Church. While in Germany, I was led to start a ministry in Enkenbach-Alsenborn and pastored for 3 years and in Bitburg, Germany for 5 years serving the men and women primarily of military communities while engaging with local German citizens. After the military I served for many years with Pastor Freddie R. at Center for Restoration in Ruskin, Florida. COVID has greatly affected fellowship amongst churches and although I remain in contact with churches, I now spend most of my time sharing the Gospel face-to-face with those in need and contributing financially to ministry and people as led. I am yet walking the path and watching and waiting for what "happeneth" next in my spiritual walk with God. Meanwhile, I serve everyday and my most prominent ministry now is to my wife, family, and mother whom I have committed to care of for the rest of her life.

The company God laid upon my heart to start in 2015 while living in Enkenbach-Alsenborn, Germany for the second time, this time as a civilian employee for the Department of Defense at Ramstein AB, Success Beyond Boundaries Enterprises, LLC is now the platform to share the love of God to my teammates. It is such a Blessing to be able to share earnings with those who help me serve the Prime customers of Amazon. Additionally, God has equipped me with the wisdom to teach Godly principles in business terminology. The slogan of the company is "Speaking things into Existence." This company name represents the vision not only of the company but of my life. I pray that everything that I do and say that upbuilds the Kingdom of God reaches beyond the extent of my imagination to affect people and the world for the good. I am grateful for my parents Arthur Barnes and Mae Frances Williams for requiring me to go to church to learn about the God of Abraham, Isaac, and Jacob. Two songs that have always inspired me are Reverend Wilson's favorite song he would sing before his sermons, "Do You Know the Man?" and Pastor I.'s favorites "All Day Long, I've Been with Jesus" or "Satan I Put You Out of My Life." My top three recording artists that can get me to the mountain top in one note is the late Reverend Timothy W., Pastor John P. K., and Bishop Hezekiah W. Our church had the pleasure of hosting concerts for the community with Reverend Timothy W. and Dawkins and D. while pastoring in Bitburg. I also had the pleasure of producing two Gospel CDs that shall ring praises towards heaven eternally…"Exodus and Lighthouse."

You may serve another God or have another source of inspiration. I cannot say that I am totally OK with that, but one tie breaker would be to request that you do not serve yourself. Our inspiration must be to serve and or uplift others as we walk through life. Companies now promote terms like team and family to signify that no man is an island. I must admit that I needed help coming into the world and will certainly need help leaving; therefore, I humble myself to realize I need help in the middle. Our nation was founded upon Godly principles that it appears we have forgotten. America must be careful least we be consumed because of our pride and reliance upon money. 2 Chronicles 7:14 reads, "If my people, which are called by my name, shall humble themselves, and pray, and seek my face, and turn from their wicked ways, then will I hear from heaven, and will forgive their sin, and will heal their land." This Scripture will speak to a nation and a person. I have personally struggled with marriage and divorce. I dearly regret that I experienced divorce as a child and that I also subjected my own children to this stressful process. I pray God will break this curse and Bless each of my children's marriages until death do them part. I learned that grief counseling could have been essential to the entire family...especially the children who are often forgotten.

I am most proud that I have introduced each of my children to Jesus Christ as well. I am so glad that this spiritual foundation has been passed to at least two generations behind me to sustain this legacy of both sides of my family. I have heard numerous stories of prisoners of war who exclaimed their survival can be attributed to either God, country, family, or the American Flag! My point, belief in a higher power than yourself is inspiration to get through tough times. I can recall an elderly church Mother in SHAPE Chapel who shared a testimony that she does not have any more bad days, but only challenging moments...that will pass. I have held on to that testimony and continue to challenge myself not to have a bad day. I encourage all to give your children a chance in this world with so many temptations and danger. Do not allow your children to become solely dependent upon you, because you do not have the power over life and death. It was important to me to teach my children how to depend on the Lord, because I knew that if we all lived a full life, one day I would have to depart and leave them behind. I have peace knowing that my children have their own relationship with God and an earthly father who loves them.

THE SOURCE...OF
INFLUENCE...PEOPLE

As human beings, at our best, we are psychologically, financially, physiologically, and spiritually balanced! As human beings, I believe we function best when connected with other humans in meaningful relationships. Working effectively with others causes us to neutralize our natural desire for selfishness and in turn, compromise, negotiate, and cooperate with others.

Psychologically, it is extremely important to manage stress through several techniques. First, we need to admit there is a little crazy in all of us especially when we are upset. Ephesians 4:26 exhorts us to be angry but not in sin. Managing our mental health is the best way in my opinion to avoid as I say, temporary insanity when we get angry. People ask me how I get so much done in a day and my response is planning and organization. This combination reduces stress because you can control what comes your way. I can recall a person getting upset with me because I asked if they would please let me know when they planned to stop by my house so I could be better prepared. The person got upset and exclaimed he felt an appointment was needed to visit me. Unless it is an emergency, yes please, let us set an appointment that is convenient for us both. I often say that one of the most difficult challenges in life is getting along with other humans. I used to watch Animal Kingdom and observed how well the animals got along and even respected the laws of the jungle. At times, I thought the animals set a better example of community than humans. I have heard that mental fatigue is worse than physical fatigue. I have witnessed people who I thought were stressed out boast how they had so much available personal leave but did not need to take it and I thought how badly they needed to take it to relieve us all. When I was working in Germany as a civilian supervisor, I appreciated the leadership of local German employees' leave. Leave was taken 3 weeks at a time each year along with other holidays throughout the year. Personally, prior to COVID-19, I planned, scheduled, and booked leave for the entire year for at least 4 weeks. This schedule was visible, exciting, a conversation piece, and something to look forward to throughout the year and kept me motivated and psychologically fit. We spend most of our alert and productive hours at work instead of with our loved ones. Planning recreational time away from work is healthy. America is wealth driven and oftentimes rest or leisure is sacrificed for the opportunity to make more money. One challenge is that we live above our means and that within itself causes daily financial stress that can bleed over into other areas of life. I taught my kids the opposite—live beneath your means and you will never be broke.

Financially, I taught my kids to use a 10-10-80 rule for financial management…10% to God, 10% to savings and investments, and live on the other 80%. However, these numbers are just for starters and can be adjusted as the financial health improves. If we live from pay day to pay day that is the equivalent of eating our seed and there is nothing left for the next harvest. I watched my Father-in-law harvest his sugar cane and then took the absolute best stalks and replanted them for the next year's harvest. As a financial advisor I had the opportunity to sit down with couples and encourage them to establish a financial get-well plan to include life insurance. Three pillars are needed: Savings, investments, and insurance. The three pillars are not optional but are crucial for family security. Do not feel bad if you do not have these pillars in place. Plan to start working towards a reasonable goal. Keep enough in your savings to cover unexpected expenses and what you invest, make sure you do not need the funds for daily expenses. I can recall speaking with a funeral director who shared that he saw people cry two times, once when their loved one died and when they found out the person was not prepared financially with insurance. In a difficult time, I had to use the services of pay day loans, but I set a goal for the duration of time, and it was worth the fee to ease a temporary stress point. Get rich over night schemes rarely work in my opinion. A solid financial plan includes a commitment to work either in an industry or as an entrepreneur. One way to create a steady flow of income is to become a river and a giver to help others. My motto is "living from my giving and giving just to live." I am not interested in creating a lake of wealth, but rather a river of flow that shall never run dry. Do your best to teach your children how to manage money. Technology has become much more advanced and more options are available for your kids. I gave my kids allowances in exchange for completing chores and making good grades and expected them to give to the church, save, and enjoy the rest.

This is where the book ends...and another begins! I woke up this morning on the final day of my first virtual family reunion, Sunday, October 3rd, 2021 and could not figure what to do at 3:00 a.m. Out of nowhere...my book came to mind and I am now motivated to complete the final chapter. The story behind the reunion is interesting as I will share the details later. I now have a writing spot that inspires my thinking and creativity. Inside of me is vision for my family and inspiration for others to unveil their vision. I was born to help others find their way... it's refreshing to discover your purpose and a challenge to live it! I have been struggling with the Scripture of taking my hands off the plow, but then I realized, I'm not only still plowing, but there are others that I have touched that are also plowing along with me. Some of my cousins for whatever reason have always inspired me by sincere questions about life, God, and many other topics that influence the way we think. Recently, I found myself conversing with my children and family members about the vision for the family...wow, what stimulating discussions to be concerned about others beyond your own lifetime. The thing that inspired me was the power of three components working together...vision to see and faith to follow! Wow…that was the key…Faith must be inclusive with vision, and without both, the people parish! If you want to follow a man's vision, he can explain every detail…and I guarantee you it will not be his best effort! However, if you want a God vision, no man can explain it all! The vision will cause you to move out in a direction and as you walk using the lamp on your feet, God will light the path before you as you walk. Along the way, you will have experiences by night, but just use the fire or challenges to inspire you to move forward as it is strengthening your faith! Along the way, you will have victories by day, this is to encourage you that the fire is working and burning off everything you don't need for the journey. Oh my God, I feel a preach coming on… Show me a time when God caused a great movement that fear was not present! Moses messed up, but the vision prevailed! David appeared to fail, but the vision prevailed! Peter denied the Man of the hour, but the vision prevailed! What about you? I declare your vision is not over…it's just beginning! Just keep walking and talking about where you are headed so the applicable people can hear it, your ears can hear it, but most of all your inner man or woman can hear it, believe it, and act upon it…because "it" WILL come to pass in DUE season! But, you must keep walking and not faint! Therefore, do not talk about your vision to just anyone, because many do not want to see that thing come to pass that in their mind will make you better than them. Small people have small thoughts. But a seasoned lady told me in plain English in the early 1980s…"son, if you want support, you got to learn how to support others!" Since that day, I can truly say…I have purposed my life to support others! And it feels good! OK, that was a commercial break…now back to writing!

GROW BEYOND your FEELINGS – COURAGE FOR THE PROFESSIONAL

ADULT EDUCATION...
NO KIDS ALLOWED

Margaret Mead as quoted in AZ Quotes (n.d.) eloquently said, "Children must be taught how to think, not what to think." This reminds me of a truth I always instilled in my children regarding problem solving. I learned in counseling others to allow them to talk through their situation, listen, and ask questions to help them navigate through their challenge. Eventually, people will arrive at their own solutions which are more effective because it was their own idea. Once my children became of age, I stopped making decisions for them, but rather helped them explore options and provided them with information that enabled them to make a better decision. The process and system of education is a foundation to learning and life itself. I could have easily been a straight "A" student, but I was no longer interested in education when my parents separated. However, the system of education had been deeply instilled in me through Sunday School and public school, so I believed the importance of obtaining my high school diploma. In high school, I was able to basically show up for most classes, pay attention, rarely submit homework, but score well on the test to pass courses and still managed to complete credit requirement 6 months early. I am not proud of my high school completion plan, but it got me through a tough period as a kid. In retrospect, in my mind, I accepted responsibility for my own decisions and life during my latter high school years. Parents who struggle with relationship challenges…do not overlook the grief your children will experience. Prioritize your child's emotional and spiritual needs and get professional help so they can make it through those challenging times.

The Work...in Securing the Right Job

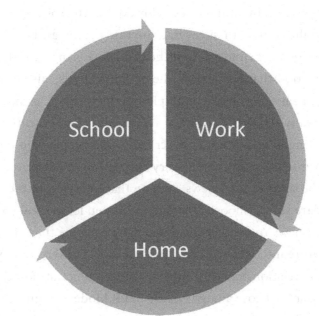

3-Peace Employee-Person (3PEP) Model (Steve Barnes)

I have learned as a Human Resources Manager that it is extremely important for the employee to be a match for the position and leadership applied for as well as the position and organization a match for the employee.

The skill set is only the beginning, but the lifestyle, attitude, and even the hidden motivation can be a distraction to mission success! The "3PEP" Model is a snapshot of who we really are in life and we are constantly transforming into something great or just "something" that people have to tolerate. The model extends through a lifetime! Just think about it… we often run to our childhood when we think about home; however, that was just the beginning and perhaps our first home. What is your home life like now? I guarantee you it has an affect on your attitude at work and general happiness with life right now. Furthermore, how you feel about home and the environment you have established has an affect on those who live with you. If you are a supervisor, leader, or business owner, develop the skill of getting people to loosen up and talk. The interviewee will begin to unravel and leak valuable information that you should not ethically ask about in an interview. However, in the spirit of the law, you have the right to remain silent and anything said can be used against you. Therefore, in the interview, if the candidate brings information into the conversation that reveals who he or she really is…listen intensively. Many organizations conduct multiple interviews to determine who the employee really is before they make a hiring decision. I mentioned earlier in this writing how one writer described some people who put on their God uniforms and go to church every Sunday out of religious habit. Well, many do the same in interviews…put on that interview outfit and put on a show. I dare you to choose different outfits and let the real you show up for the interview! You will be amazed at how knowing the real you will go to every future interview will change your daily conversation, your daily habits, your relationship with others, your conduct at home, and your overall character! Close analysis of the 3PEP Model can guide the person and the employer to good decision making. Focus on the 3PEP Model can help you develop and reach goals in a balanced manner. Once hired, involvement in your employee's personal and professional goals in life strengthens a positive relationship and partnership! What's really going on here? Honesty and transparency. The 3PEP model helps the mentor to help the mentee. Employers, if you don't want people to leave you, stop being selfish and create a reason and a way for them to stay, grow, and develop! Otherwise, make sure you have a succession plan for the expected stay of your hires. If people are leaving too fast and too often…change something about the culture!

Be Strong and of A Good Courage – The Conclusion of the Matter

ACQUIRING ANOTHER
SPIRIT...REBRANDING

Forgive me for not remembering the actual author, but I was inspired by the thought...many people never reach their full potential, because they reach a certain place and get comfortable and stop striving for self-actualization. That statement has been a push in my life. I have done so many things in my life and realize I'm a straight dare man--not devil! LOL I can look back and see how it all happened. I can look back over my life and remember swinging on a vine across a pitch-black pond with branches sticking out and no doubt full of moccasin snakes at the dare of my friends. After I conquered the dare and made it back to shore, my friends had the courage to follow, and the pond turned into a regular meeting place. I can remember my mom saying to my brother that he would follow me off a cliff! I guess I have always had an influence on others somehow...I realize I have the gift of exhortation and love motivational speaking...I hope this is my next rebranding! I want to share my story and help somebody! I want to have an influence on small business owners and employees, I want to help those struggling with bad habits, I want to help those who have been incarcerated get a new start, I have helped people all over the world and now I want to help my family, and finally, I want to help all those that God leads my way. I recall being on a bus ride to school and the kids gave the 10 second challenge and then hold your breath. Well, I watched several bus riders hold their breath at the count of 10 but they chickened out and started breathing with a big gasp. Well, yours truly stepped up and said, "I can do it!" I remember holding my breath and wanting to breathe, but I decided to go all the way to see what would happen! Well, perhaps this was about the 10th time God had spared my life, because I totally blacked out! When I came back around, I was on the floor on my back looking up at scared faces looking at me. I had no clue why I was on the floor and why they were looking at me. I don't know how long I was out, but I figured I shouldn't ever try that one again! Growing up we watched professional wrestling a lot and of course, we had wrestling matches amongst ourselves. Although we were warned not to try those moves at home…we did! I can recall my scariest experience, while waiting after school one day this fella made me mad, and I put him in the sleeper hold around his throat and head. Just like on television he started fighting frantically to get loose, but the more he fought against me, the tighter I clamped down. Just like on television, he started slowing down and eventually went limp…then I got scared because he passed out just like I did on that floor in the bus. I didn't think to call for help, I just calmly sat him up, rubbed the back of his neck and shoulders like I saw the wrestlers do, and hit him forcefully in the back of the head and neck area and he suddenly came back to life! What a sigh of relief…another thing I figured I better not try again. Fast forwarding, I recall graduating early from high school, working a full-time and part-time job, getting my own car, paying my bills and helping mom, and I figured I was a man…at 17 years of age. One night, I decided to stay out all night, and of course, mom was a single parent and going crazy looking for me. When we met up at home, she told me to go join the Army because I was not going to behave in that manner at her house. Well, the old dare boy decided to take her up on her word; however, since Vietnam was in full force, I decided I better not join the Army, but I did join the Air Force. At my first virtual family reunion, I learned that was the same reason my Uncle Charlie joined the Air Force! Now as I look back at my mom's statement, why would she send me to the Army at that time? Oh my! Let me move on… This was my first true rebranding!

God used the Air Force to save my life…again! I had several near-death experiences as a teenager and just before leaving for the Air Force I fell asleep driving home and crashed my car about 500 feet from the Florida Highway Patrol Office and missed a utility pole by inches. Commercial break…a sleep driver is worse than a drunk driver! Basic training was a breeze for me because I was raised in the South and had endured multiple beat downs at home and many fights because I was the oldest and didn't have any help! My claim to fame is nobody fought me twice…win or lose! Too much work because I never gave up and if I could get up, the fight was not over! I guess that is the same attitude that has turned into a positive in my life…if you don't give up, you can't lose…because it's not over! I do believe there is some crazy in all of us…it just takes the right situation to bring it out. I certainly did some growing up in the Air Force and was exposed to many things and a different way of life that changed my life! The rebranding was the whole person concept! Success in the Air Force required three things: Outstanding at your job; contributor to the military base and surrounding community; self-improvement! During my Air Force years, I coined the phrase, "Living from my giving, and giving, just to live." The source is Luke 6:38, "Give, and it shall be given unto you; good measure, pressed down, and shaken together, and running over, shall men give into your bosom. For with the same measure that ye mete withal it shall be measured to you again." If I stop giving, I stop living.

3P Life Model (Steve Barnes)

One of the most disgusting things I have ever seen is selfish people who think of no one or thing above themselves as they navigate through life. The only time when selfish people help others is when it is convenient or creates an audience for more self-praise. I learned in Sunday School to treat others as you want to be treated and to love your neighbor, as yourself. The Air Force reinforced this gesture with core values that were instilled in me: "Integrity First, Service Before Self, and Excellence in all we do!" (Ball, 2021) The 3P Model is how I have resolved to live out the rest of my life...and have been for decades! I have learned that in helping others...I'm helping myself so it's no harm in putting myself last...so it appears! In Luke, when Jesus was speaking about workers of iniquity, etc. in Chapter 13 and verse 30, He concluded the dialogue with "And, behold, there are last which shall be first, and there are first which shall be last." There you have the 3P Model reaffirmed...YOU focus on the purpose that you contribute to this world (your job, trade, mission, vision, etc.), serve others within your family and community, and seek self-improvement outside of yourself! It will take you a lifetime to complete the 3P Model. This is the only way you will ever reach your self-actualization in the Maslow Hierarchy of Needs! Cherry (2021) shared in the article on Maslow's Hierarchy of Needs as a theory of human behavior. Allow me to interject, although I agree with these influences on human behavior, we must keep this behavior in perspective of the 3P Model. In fact, the Air Force allowed me to experience each level of the pyramid from providing means for my basic needs through pay and benefits, a safe environment to work and play, the camaraderie of my fellow Airmen, self-esteem through awards and recognition, and finally promotion throughout the ranks as far as I desired. However, although this pyramid helps me understand why I and others behave the way we do… it's the self-esteem to self-actualize that gets us in trouble with selfishness! Proverbs 27:2 declares, "Let another man praise thee, and not thine own mouth; a stranger, and not thine own lips." If you are that great…someone else will recognize it and give you a shout out! However, when we strive for the shout out instead of the mission and support of those around us…it leads to disappointment and discouragement. Over a period, this disappointment and discouragement turns into low self-esteem, depression and leads to other undesirable things to include a selfish perspective of Maslow's Hierarchy.

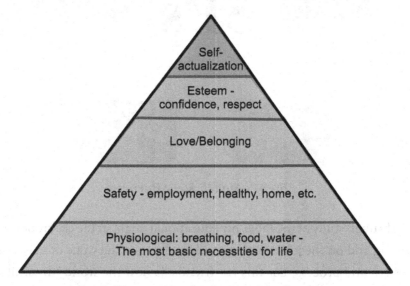

Basic Human Needs. Source: Pixabay.com

Through this rebranding with the Air Force I was drawn out of self and realized a larger purpose beyond myself. I was a dad suddenly at 18 years of age and oh boy was that another life changer that helped start my transition into adulthood. By choice and not force, this is where I began to learn the value of putting others before myself. Matter of fact, from this point my life was focused on raising my children and creating a safe home to project them as a launching pad into this world equipped for the dangers to come. I firmly believe that challenges, or fire, drives us to where we need to be in life. We would never ask for these challenges if it were our choice, but when we make the best of those challenges and work through them, we become better people on the other side.

The 5Ps Model, Steve Barnes

Through study of the Bible, my educational plight in the classroom, and training and on the job experience, I have learned the value of mastering a system and process. For this my friends, is how the world turns…it's a system and process. There is a system and for it to operate at its optimum, the process must occur…repeatedly. My 5P Model is my system and process and approach to the Purpose, People, and my Person—3Ps! Be prompt! I was taught the early bird gets the worm at home. In the military, it was hurry up...and wait! In other words, show up before the appointed time, and wait to be called upon. If you are not early...you are late! Being on time shows respect for others and I find that people that are continuously late have a broken system and process. Furthermore, if you are consistently late...you are thinking too highly of yourself and not considerate of others. Take a moment to think about all the people who are late in your life...why? A Bible story comes to mind about the five wise and five foolish virgins who awaited the bridegroom. The Marine 5Ps say "Prior Preparation Prevents Poor Performance!" (author unknown) Promptness is a statement about you and your seriousness about what you are doing.

Precision deals with studying your craft and being the best at it! I remember the words of Dr. Martin Luther King, Jr. as he exalted men and women to be the best at their purpose in life! If it's street sweeping...be the best! I can recall teaching my kids how to sweep a porch or room...a system and process! You have to herd that trash as a cattleman herds the cattle. Organize whatever you are doing, and you will be amazed at the result. Before you start moving and working and doing things...spend a few minutes thinking about the approach to the task. Develop a goal, and then begin the task. Remember, this is the NGB Model...needs, behavior, and goal! We do this repeatedly in our daily lives...so why not perfect that process?

Professionalism is a must in the workplace. I can recall some lessons from my high school Future Business Leaders of America training. We were taught everything from dining etiquette to the importance of eye contact and how to dress. Our visual presentation and impression on others speak louder than the words we speak. Our response to unprofessionalism defines our professionalism. Again...challenges and tough situations will come your way, but it is your opportunity to self-check your growth! How you respond defines where you are in that area of challenge. As a child, I repeated the phrase sticks and stones may break my bones, but words will never hurt me. I found that statement to be false as an adult, and as a child...the phrase was just a coping mechanism. Amazingly, as a Human

Resources Manager, I still see these childish games being played in the workplace! Rebranding requires renewing your mind and departing from nonproductive activity and behavior and embracing purpose (my 2022 theme) with every decision and action. Reaching goals is a series of related decisions leading one through milestones along the way. Force yourself to know why you are doing things!

My Amazon Story

I have always been an entrepreneur as I look back at playing Monopoly everyday throughout summers and learning how to wheel and deal. No matter who I played against, I always seemed to find a way to win the game with very few losses. According to Mom, this led to my creativity in school selling comic books, trading for personal possessions, selling hot toothpicks, and much more I probably should not discuss in writing. Later I began acquiring yards to cut and rake on a regular basis...I had a lawnmower and gas can and walked the neighborhood and earned my spending money. Our parents taught us to pick pecan and sell them and just become resourceful not looking for handouts but learning to embrace the values of hard work. The willingness to work was evident to my Dad and Grandfather as I began to accompany them on their jobs.

From hunting, to fishing, to mowing the grass, to car repair and maintenance, to delivering packages on a delivery van I was always learning how to do something. After leaving home these skills were invaluable and helped me save lots of money in my home and on my cars. I thought it was so cool to ride in the delivery van with the door open and I was the runner of packages to the door of customers around the city. Meanwhile, my Grandfather was a plumber and I was his apprentice. As you can guess, I did all the dirty work and as I look back...quite dangerous! When we are young, we tend to be brave and have little fear of things in general. At least that is my story as you can recall earlier in the book. At the house, my Grandfather had a host of chores to teach me as well ranging from farming, to plowing, to picking fruit, to slaughtering hogs, and so much more. I don't know why, but work was not hard…it was interesting. My mind was always naturally churning in a business sense as I was exposed to various tasks and situations. For example, after helping my Grandfather on a job at people's houses, I would negotiate jobs raking or mowing lawns of his plumbing customers. I would go hunting sometimes with Dad and sometimes with my Grandfather and eventually went solo. You guessed it…I would give some of my kill away and some I sold. I remember money was tight and for some of my years Mom was a single parent and things got worse financially. I am grateful for the work ethics I saw and developed as a child because I attribute that to never being hungry! The entire neighborhood worked together and I witnessed the result of the camaraderie and teamwork… everybody shared their harvest and no one lacked! Some had grapes, some corn, some peas, some cows, some hogs, some chickens, and the list goes on, but there was a time to work and a time to eat.

The culmination of these experiences stayed with me no matter where I travelled in the military, and I always desired to own my business. I was always on the watch for that break, that moment, that opportunity to start a business. When I least expected that opportunity…it presented itself! My love for driving around with Dad in that moving truck matured into me owning a logistical business delivering packages. Here lies another important concept to remember…know how to connect dots for why you are doing things. Where did your dream or goals begin? Remembering the time and place adds strength, commitment, believability, and success to your endeavor! It was no accident or fluke, but hard work, drive and energy, and perseverance.

In 2015, while living in Germany, I woke up one day and told my wife it was time to start the company! Of course, I'm sure she thought I was crazy, but I was sure God woke me up to get started as if I was going into business the following week. After much prayer, meditation, deliberation, and discussion, we settled on the initials that has become my A.K.A. sign— SBB! Just as naming your child takes much thought…so did this business name. Words matter and can inspire or tear down. The name that was birth was Success Beyond Boundaries! This was the mission of what we aimed to do and the vision of where and how far we wanted to go! Once we captured the name of the company we incorporated something I firmly believe in…that is, speaking things into existence. Romans 4:17 declares, "…and calleth those things which be not as though they were!" Speak your dream! Allow your heart to feel the vibration of your words! Allow your ears to hear your words…in your voice…repeatedly until your mind believes you mean business! Next, you must be able to envision what you say! Write it on paper or draw a picture! This was the point where I searched for help in designing the picture that would remind me of this dream and vision. I found Allen and we connected immediately! Check out what we did through collaboration!

Allen and I talked and emailed one another repeatedly until we were both satisfied on every detail of the picture that would represent now…and then! Although I was in Germany, Allen was in Florida. This also made me feel good since I am a Floridian and planned on moving back to the Greater Tampa, Florida area. By now you can see that I walk by Faith…and not by sight! Speak something that is not…into existence is what literally happens as I hear the story of so many that are doing something great! From the star sports athlete to the movie star—start dreaming early and talk about that dream. As parents, stir up conversation and see what is on the young minds. We started doing business, researching ideas, talking to people, but didn't know how the business would look. We eventually returned to Florida and continued this plight for another 2 years…then it happened! Allow me to interject a thought, many people say they pray, but when the answer to the prayer appears…they do not recognize it because it does not look exactly as they expected "in the natural." Prayer is spiritual and you must look in your visionary mind to see the results first and then watch them develop in the natural. Perhaps you heard the story about the man who was stranded on an island and needed a rescue! He began to pray to God for help! Soon after a helicopter showed up, but the man refused to get on because he was waiting on God! A ship showed up, but the man refused to climb aboard because he was determined to wait on God! In desperation the man cried out to God…"where are you?" God answered, "I sent you a helicopter and a ship, but you refused to leave!

While teaching one afternoon in an online course my wife approached me with an Amazon website soliciting delivery service partners! I read the ad and immediately…I knew this was the answer to my prayer, the engine for Success Beyond Boundaries, and my opportunity to bring my dream into full fruition. I shut down my course work and immediately started completing my application and accompanying requirements and I was done within a couple of hours. Everything flowed so easily because I had documents on my computer, thoughts in my head, and a vision for every question asked. Timing is extremely important in many facets! There is a time to sow and a time to reap. A time to study and a time to work. A time to laugh and a time to cry. When the opportunity avails itself…you must have already done the homework and be ready to capitalize and seize the moment! I can recall working with a Pastor in Germany and I shall never forget the words he spoke to me with tears in his eyes…he said, "you gave me what no other person had ever given me…opportunity!" Opportunity is not a question but deserves a response! Dare…I say Dare…to possess a good courage! I leaped at this chance to give life to my logo and decided I would go all the way! I had no clue what was to come…but because of my heightened courage and anticipation of launching the business to the next level, I figured I needed to go all the way! Once a person holds his breath until he collapses what else does it take to prove courage? I was that guy! After one year of stressful interviews, it all worked out!

My joy in running the business is using all the tools, training, education, and experiences of my life and career up to that point! Everything is a resource to include the most difficult moments and people…they prepare you for the now! Leading people is challenging but rewarding for both the leader and the follower. This point on leadership assumes the leader is prepared for the task at hand. Effective leadership in a professional environment requires some form of training or education, practice, and experience. I get joy when people get promoted within my company and I love to see the confused expression on their faces when I also inform them of the requirement to humble themselves and serve others. This is in direct contrast to the leader's expectation of elevation and respect from others. This is my version of "upside-down leadership structure."

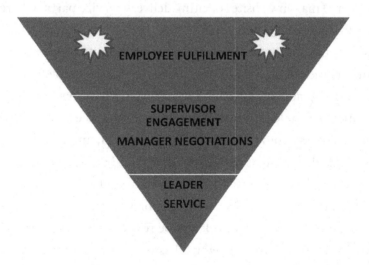

Upside-Down Leadership Structure (SBB)

As simple as it may seem, in America, people want to achieve and succeed and become an icon that people worship. America is about the haves or have nots. Bottom line if you have lots of money you will inevitably have lots of friends. Therefore, if you are in charge, you expect people to give you special respect. Some people call this brown-nosing...it is a common practice to move up in the organizational chain; therefore, once you are there you expect others to do the same. I declare it is time to break that chain with SBB Upside Down Organizational Structure. Whatever your business that makes you money, I hope you would agree that employees are your most valuable resource. I will admit that my model assumes you value people. Whether a one-way dictator style leader or the opposite, a servant-minded leader, both must have people to get the mission done. The dictator is more position power oriented and that does not take a whole lot of thought—I'm in charge and you do what I say, or you are fired! Let's focus on the servant leader who values people's worth and feelings and leads firmly but respectfully. At the base of the model, the leader is responsible for gathering all the resources necessary to make the supervisor and employee successful if used properly. Look beyond the obvious of raw materials...I believe this might be one challenge for small businesses. You must consider the human factor touch points in operating a successful business...training, coaching, communication, and objective feedback. I soon realized that my managerial staff had technical know how for the business functions but lacked the ability to "lead" the team in various situations. The managerial staff expected drivers to do what they said because they were in charge. For some time, the managers were able to ride on my wings...do this or that or I will have to turn you in to Mr. Steve! I disliked this approach and considered it a cop out! As the leader, I had started weekly sessions with the managerial staff lasting 2 hours—one hour devoted to mission and one hour devoted to leadership! Once the foundation was laid after about a year, I was able to reduce the time to one hour. Outside of the weekly sessions, I had established a common vocabulary so I could coach managers individually in short bursts to be more specific pending the team role. Managers were encouraged to express their true opinions to the leader that reflected the concerns, interests, and complaints of the supervisors and team members. Managers learned the whys from the leader and were able to provide the middle ground for the supervisors and drivers that they had direct contact.

Supervisors deliver the daily task requirements to the employees or team members. While the managers were growing into leadership capable, the supervisors still struggled. Greater investment in the supervisors was also required just as with the managers. Supervisors required training on how to handle disgruntled employees or drivers. Lesson one is realizing you are promoted to serve and not be served! Accept upside down thinking and you automatically will be able to withstand a greater degree of unwanted behavior from subordinates. Employees are the recipients of the best that leadership collectively has to offer. Employees must feel fulfilled at each level of leadership to really buy into the organization's purpose for existence. I remember hiring a driver once who was captured on video delivering for another company doing terrible things. After a one-on-one interview with the driver, establishment of a mutual understanding, I hired the driver, and he did an outstanding job for our team! He told me that he did those things with his previous employer because they did not care for him nor respect him. I spent targeted time and conversations with the new teammate to prove the company was indeed what was presented in the interview. Employees must feel the love at each echelon of the organization to believe it is wholesome. Leaders must become interested in what is important to employees…that interest extends beyond money. I believe the misperception of money power is the crime committed most often against employees. The SBB Upside Down Organizational Structure provides daily reminders to leaders to be concerned about the well being of employees— financially, psychologically, and physically. The leader must remain in touch regularly with every level of leadership and the employees. One of the rewards of this structure is employees are raised in this environment and as they grow they can help strengthen the model when they become leaders.

As a drill instructor, part of the motivation to lead came from smelling brand new uniforms sometimes saturated with the sweat of the San Antonio heat and humidity, or hearing the unified heel beat of 50 marching men rattling the dormitory or looking an airman in the eyes and knowing that one more breakdown could send him over the edge. Leaders need to remain in touch with reality and not just stare at manufactured reports that indicate they are great! People do not care unless they know you care! I get joy and pride when I can go on a delivery route and use the same tools as the team, get wet in the rain, or sweat like a hog before the slaughter in the middle of the Florida summer heat. I can then better relate to the concerns of the team or poor excuses with no substance. Leadership is so creative and almost like putting together a puzzle where the shapes are made as you engage. Take the time to get to know each person you desire to lead... even if it is your child—I have learned this is the epitome of leadership! Do not give up!

Unfortunately, I have hired teammates that had visible scars from previous employment and seemingly no or poor leadership. The negative attitude, worthless demeanor, and inconsistent work is a usual reflection of lack of effective leadership. I welcome these opportunities to practice leadership! My motivation stays high because of the starfish story—I cannot lose if I improve just one person! The story goes a man was walking along a beach and picking up starfish that had washed ashore and tossing them back into the ocean. Someone challenged the man and scorned him for wasting his time tossing starfish back into the ocean and not making a difference. As the man tossed another one, he exclaimed, "I made a difference for that one." Effective leadership begins with the leader being confident with his or her own strengths and weaknesses. Leadership is merely helping someone get better! I recently asked our company leaders to rank order five entities we interact with daily: Self, customers we serve, our team, our drivers, or our parent contracted company. I received various versions, but no one listed the entities in my desired order. My list has our driver as the number one concern! Why might you ask? Because as the owner of the company/team, I do not see the customers—the driver does! Therefore, the driver is our internal customer that must be satisfied to in turn, satisfy our external customers. I ask our leaders to place the team or company as #2! I'm glad you asked why! As the leader, I employ the SBB Upside Down Organizational Structure and ensure our representative who faces the customer is fulfilled to the reasonable expectation. Within this individual are the core values of the company which are the 5Ps mentioned earlier, Prompt, Precise, Professional, Preventative, and Positive. If team members value the company they will exceed Amazon and the external customer's needs. As leadership, I focus on the contracted customer and when that customer is satisfied, the external customer is also satisfied. Thirdly, I train our leaders to focus on our contracted customer for the reason previously mentioned. Why is this customer third and not second you may ask? The managers and supervisors are paid by me—not the contracted customer. As requirements and changes are communicated to me as the leader, I in turn communicate how our team will adjust and perform work. Fourthly, leaders focus on the external customer in those times where there may be a problem with a team member/driver. The manager can step in and negotiate or become that buffer to ensure a good outcome or refer the issue to myself as the leader. Finally, as supervisors and managers who have authority and position power, they must always put themselves last in consideration as depicted by our upside-down model. The team members have limited ability to defend themselves on the job so I as the leader protect them through the upside-down model to ensure they receive proper treatment and respect. The preferred order of precedence for the supervisor and manager focus is the driver (team member), Success Beyond Boundaries, contracted company, external customer, and finally self! The desired characteristics of effective leaders embody humility, unselfishness, and simply putting the concerns of others before your own. This is the recipe for earning respect from others. I can place supervisors and managers in a position but they must earn the respect for authority on their own from the team through earnest and consistent concern for others.

Out of the Mouth of Babes...Mature Age

I promised earlier not to make this a Christian book, but I must call your attention to the simplicity of God and His Word as expressed in Psalms 8 and the latter part of Matthew 11. In other words, some of the most powerful lessons of wisdom and knowledge are very simple...to the point that those who claim to be super smart miss the facts of life! The Gospel writer further complicate this point in 1 Corinthians 13:1, "When I was a child, I spake as a child, I understood as a child, I thought as a child: but when I became a man, I put away childish things." I cannot tell you the number of times I have witnessed men and women have temper tantrums as if they were toddlers because things were not going their way. In a professional environment, I have witnessed people yelling to the top of their lungs, stomping out of rooms, slamming things on the desk, all because things were not going their way. Again, I point us back to childhood where we learned how to sway people our way. I was extremely mindful of raising my kids in their childhood because of habits that would be formed. I didn't have a book to raise kids by so at 18 years old I had to figure it out and I chose logic! I found ways to increase the likelihood for my kids to sleep all night...reduced their daytime naps. LOL Wake up little Jr, wake up little momma...it's not bedtime yet! By the time I was sleepy...the baby was like thank God that fool is gone now I can get some rest! I used logic! At a certain time in the evening, I reduced drinks for toddlers to help them not wet the bed. Logic…last stop before bed was the toilet and the first stop in the morning was the toilet. Out of the mouth of babes the enemy is confounded. I can recall disciplining one of my children about getting trouble in school in kindergarten or first grade. We had a great do not do it again session and I felt accomplished! Leadership! The next day we had the same problem, and I was confounded as the enemy! I'm thankful that before I engaged in another disciplining session, I asked the babe…why did you do it again? The response I received was so simple, but so powerful that I still live by those words today! My child responded, "because I wanted to." Initially, that made me even more angry, but in processing what was said I was paralyzed in thought! I didn't like the answer, but it was me that asked the question. That response ended the disciplining session and it turned into a wisdom lesson for me…as a parent, as a leader, as a human being I do not have the power to make anyone do anything! God gave us all a will! Wow! From that day I began to officially practice leadership!

As a leader in my upside-down model, I realize that employees at the top of the pyramid possess valuable information that I need to help make decisions. Creating an environment where employees feel safe and can speak without retribution, is invaluable for the leadership and organization. The most complex challenges within the organization can be resolved because the employees are closest to the customer or issue. My child taught me that I can hire employees, but I cannot make them do what I want them to do. I must find a way to nurture them to become mature contributing partners on the team. However, throughout that process I must feed them with wholesome foods and balanced diets called training, education, corrective feedback, communication, praise, and rewards. One way to protect the company is to develop metrics and safety measures to indicate when something is going wrong to minimize the damage. I propose a better way is to observe and take advantage of opportunities to commend good work and creative ideas that can be developed and incorporated into the organization. I cannot express in words how this motivates employees! Remember, leaders cannot motivate people, rather, people must choose to become motivated. Therefore, my job as a leader is to ensure the ground is fertile with things that help the employees choose to be motivated rather than something else! I make time to give one-on-one time with as many team members as possible as often as possible and listen to what they have to say; usually, I'm able to gleam something that can help the team, help me, or reveal how I can help the team member specifically. Again, I say when people feel you sincerely care for them you will be amazed at what they can give to the team. I believe in people! Yes, people hurt each other but people also help each other more often. No man is an island! As babes need help, it reflects how we will always need help no matter what stage of life we reach! This is the thought concept that keeps me humble and respectful of others…we need each other!

When I speak with children or new employees, I am especially attentive as they drop powerful messages and opportunities for growth and improvement. As adults or senior employees with a team we can get easily complacent. This complacency can become harmful to the team because I firmly believe every decade, major change occurs all around and within you! Yes, think about when you went from 10 to 20 years old! Remember, from 20 to 30…the first sign of heck I'm getting old! I can recall joining the Air Force and taking my typing test on a manual typewriter. You could only type so fast because you had to go to the gym to work out your fingers to be able to push the keys down hard enough to put the ink on the paper. Oh boy, then we graduated to electric typewriters. About 10 years into the Air Force, they were pushing the first computer at me, and all my peers joined me in saying we don't like Peachtree and Enable! Why? Because those programs represented change and we were comfortable in our baby stage. However, after we were forced, I meant encouraged to learn the new programs you couldn't separate us from them. The babes my friend help prepare us for what is to come! It is in our best interest to watch and observe what interests and attracts them because we will surely have to deal with it as the enemy reflected in the Scriptures mentioned earlier in Psalms 8 and Matthew 11. I raised my first child at 18 years old. I had my last child when I was 32 years old. At almost twice the age I had learned a lot about kids and life and was much better at parenting through trial and error. As I raised this last child, I realized so many things had changed from the first and in some cases, things were easier and in others more challenging. This last child helped me grasp some changes in society and I can recall a defining moment before we reached the time of acceptance of all people regardless of their choices. At this time, my child had friends of the opposite sex who preferred relationships with people of the same sex. In a conversation one day my daughter asked me why I wasn't as accepting to some of her friends and once again I became paralyzed in thought, because I needed something very profound as a parent to say. The words never came. Soon after as my child got older and became drawn to piercing and tattoos I thought I had lost the war because remember my other child taught me there was nothing I could do to stop the child from loving those tats and things! Well, I just had to take one shot at change and exclaimed you will never get a good job with all that going on. You must know not only did the child get the job but several promotions as well. Out of the mouth of babes…we can grow tremendously and gain great wisdom! God uses the simple…to confound the wise! I'm sure I shared this earlier, but this is a good time to reinforce… everything I needed to know and practice now as an adult…I learned as a child!

As we grow older, we should mature and put away childish things as shared in First Corinthians previously. As a child, we cried to get what we wanted and if we are still yelling and crying to get what we want…that is a problem. I see far too many senior leaders using this tactic along with the power of their office to get their way! Negotiating and communicating with subordinates is beneath those type leaders and they rule by force, but rarely can they expect true loyalty. This is a good point in this manuscript to look within yourself and decide to make some changes…that only you can make! Why? Glad you asked! Like it or not, you are getting older, and the saying goes, "once a man or woman and twice a child." I am noticing my surroundings and notice people that do not prepare for the end of their career and end of life struggle terribly with humbling themselves to receive needful help! I see the effect on caregivers and specialized staff that is committed to a service for a disgruntled person that forgot to prepare for the change after all those decades of warning. Do you recall the movie Benjamin Buttons where life was reversed? Although we are in grown up bodies, if we live a full life, we should get ready to need daily care from someone! Make sure you are likable and tolerable before you reach that point. I'm winding down now with the conclusion of the whole matter—I dare you to possess a good courage...even in the face of death! Start now and get counsel on preparing for the end of things...empty nest, career, and life itself. Good preparation reduces negative stress, enhances positive stress, and grants one peace with self, others, and the situation at hand. Allow me some things to throw your way in the way of homework for you to get done now, before it is too late!

The baby needs finances, substance, shelter, security, care giver, and some form of spiritual support. Out of the mouth of babes...comes the simplicity of life! Let me save some ink right here and share my top 10 with you in no particular order: 1) Stop living on a full pay check and live off no more than 80% and save/invest at least 10% and give the other 10% to church/charity; 2) Get a will, executor you can trust, a trust, and healthcare surrogate; 3) Evaluate and secure insurance needs...life and health; 4) Plan for retirement budget and activities; 5) Do not depend on your children to take care of you in old age...let that be plan B or C; get a solid plan A to ride life out into the sunset; 6) Connect with God personally and not via the church or another person; 7) Replace work plans with volunteerism and enriching activities that cause brain and limb function...start before you get there; 8) Eliminate debt except the essentials and live on cash rule—if you don't have the cash you can't afford it; 9) Seek wise counsel, hang out with positive people, and limit time with negativism in all forms; 10) Live everyday to the fullest and don't put off too many things for tomorrow! I hear you...saying but I cannot afford to do all those things. Yes you can, I taught you how to do it..."start speaking things into existence." Just keep saying what you want then you will find yourself believing, seeing, and ultimately doing! You can do it! Reminder...no man is an island! This is not a Christian book but let me slip one more thing in that everyone can benefit, Philippians 4:13 says, "I can do all things through Christ which strengtheneth me." KJV I will admit to you that until I was close to 30 I sincerely thought investing was for only the rich! When I finally sat down with a financial advisor, with limited resources at the time, I could not account for $600 monthly! I knew I made it but didn't know where I spent it. I was embarrassed and that was the start of my plight to start my top 10 list previously mentioned. I hope to write more about some of the top 10 in another manuscript, but for now I wanted you to start thinking about change…in your life now for a better future! I do it through Christ, but just get beyond yourself…there is safety in the multitude! Remember, out of the mouth of babes…that's why back in our school days there were gang fights! People tend to feel safer and more protected and more assured to win…in the multitude! I can have a greater negative effect on a person if I can find 5 more people to isolate that person and not associate with them. Not all childish things are positive and those are the ones we should avoid. However, I'm sure you have seen this same behavior in adults, and I'm sometimes embarrassed for them. Put away childish things and get ready to enjoy every moment of life to include the end when you know you have maximized the years God gave you on this earth! Well, if you will not listen to those babes, life is not so gentle!

MY GREATEST TEACHER...LIFE

Oh boy! I wish I had the time to tell you about all the lessons I have learned in the ugly detail in which they occurred! Let me start this portion of the book with an apology to all whom I have caused harm through my ignorance, disobedience, and stubbornness of navigating through life! I learned the power of the will from my 6-year-old child! I have learned through living life that as I grow older each decade, I have reached a point where I would not take my own advice previously given. Therefore, I stopped giving advice many years ago and pushed people young and old into making their own decisions as they navigate life! Life is intended to be a personal journey but with the guidance of God and support of others. Possess a good courage and don't put what is intended for you to decide on others! I can remember making my first financial mistake that cost me about 10+ years to recover! I paid off my first car and wanted a new one even though I couldn't afford it...so I borrowed the money from a creditor. A wise man who was decades older than I encouraged me to get a $2K loan instead if I had to and do some things to the car I had to improve it, i.e., paint job. After several years of struggle, I realized I could no longer afford the car and sold it and bought a cheaper car. Decades later while living in Germany, I met a man that was my age...40s and he told me he had never borrowed money for a new car. I was all ears at this point as he explained his parents taught him to save the money for the car you wanted

and pay cash. Once you get that car, start saving for the next one! Wow…
what a "simple" concept that many miss! Once you save for that first one…
the rest is history. From that day, I vowed to eventually reach the point
where I could also buy my cars cash. All it would cost is patience. What a
lesson to start teaching our generations!

The challenge we experience in general is hurrying to grow up when we
feel life is forever and fiercely pumping the breaks after we realize we are
going to die one day. Imagine if we could engage and develop a relationship
with our babes where they would trust us through that growing up process
and slow things down. I know my parents tried to protect me from all
the things that perhaps hurt them and so did I with my kids. For some
unknown reason, children must find out the stove is hot for themselves.
Living on planet earth has changed tremendously during my decades and
is very challenging especially for youth. My brother was a Sheriff and he
used to tell his kids I would rather you listen to me as opposed to the man
or woman who will lock you up in jail. I see parents who attempt to protect
their kids from harm, firm discipline, and basically try and give the kids
everything within their spending power. Just remember, whatever you do is
creating a lifelong expectation for your children…who do you prefer giving
your kids a lesson on life? I strongly encourage parents to take a position
of "preparing" your child for life in this world. Equip your kids with life
skills, discipline, and good eating, playing, and sleeping habits. I dare you—
to possess good courage to provide these essentials to your most valued
treasure on earth! Children will ask and beg for what they "want" but you
must first meet your parental obligation to give them what they "need."

Allow me to share a couple of examples. Far too often we live in a time
where many children are raised in single parent homes—got it! I observe
and have knowledge as many children are entertained by the TV or some
electronic device for hours upon hours to keep them quiet and occupied.
I understand why, but this concerns me as these children continue these
habits and lack of supervision for years upon years. Remember, earlier I
shared how quickly values for life are locked! I have observed children with
the device in the car, in the bathroom, at the dinner table, and clutched

in bed as they fall asleep. One day, I can see Capitol Hill seats filled with the youth of today gaming while running the country. Secondly, when did we stop doing dinner with our children? I got it that parents are busy even in two parent homes; however, you have a responsibility to teach and train your children. Yes, there is a difference in teaching and training... do both! For example, who will teach your children how to eat properly? Or, will they teach themselves? Food for thought, why not take advantage of a set time that fits everyone's schedule as a time to eat together however many nights you can and let that be a time of communication and sharing. No electronics allowed. Of course, there are so many other examples and creative ways to have a positive effect on your children and prepare them for the world. I mentioned playing purposely for a way to exercise. Retirement does not mean stay at home, sit on the sofa all day with the remote, and eat yourself to death. You agree, right? So why would we do that to our children? Eating vegetables, learning to keep a clean room, proper hygiene, and regular activity time is so important to our children. Of course, the children do not know this, nor do they care...until the teacher called "life" starts talking. The Centers for Disease Control and Prevention (n.d.) reported from 1999-2000 through 2017-2018, obesity increased from 30.5% to 42.4%. You recall the budget I encouraged earlier, health cuts into the budget and illness shortens life expectancy. I am just making a point but do understand the many factors that could cause obesity. Let's call this avoidable obesity...teach and train your child either way. I am taking one for the team by mentioning these things because one day when struggling, don't give your child the alibi of blaming you for their challenges. OK here is one more for the road...do not allow kids to baby sit kids under no circumstances..."bad" things happen! I replaced the word "bad" with "challenge" for common use, but I intentionally used the word bad in this instance. Maybe the first couple of days or weeks go without a glitch but this is a time bomb waiting to go off! Look into government or state programs and reputable family to help. Set up a partnership and get creative but remember your responsibility to prepare your children from the lessons of life! I can reach back to my childhood days and associate many adult behaviors that led to unnecessary lessons in life...or were they? I believe good things come to those who wait, but sometimes while waiting a lot of things happen that are not so good. No worries. Just connect with God and experience the true meaning of love...that I found takes time and difficult challenges before you know you got it! Love may be found in good times, but it is proven in difficult times. Romans 8:28 declares, "And we know that all things work together for good to them that love God, to them who are the called according to *his* purpose." Possess the good courage and chase your purpose as your lifelong goal! Discover a purpose larger than you! Discover a purpose that will outlive you! I challenged my kids with a question while they were going to school and figuring out what to do in life: How will you help society? Now on that journey you will endure many lessons in life, but they will not be in vain but rather, filled with purpose in preparing you for something greater! In the year 2022, I challenged our team and all those who know me..."Embrace Purpose!"

If you do not think some of my examples fit you, let's listen to someone several decades older than me—what people in the 90s would say! Sohn (2019) asked one man if he had any regrets about not accomplishing more in life and he responded, "No, I wish I had loved more." Remember love just as our answered prayers are not always packaged in wrapping paper with cute bows. However, hidden within these opportunities are our lessons in life that can not only Bless ourselves, but it is enough for others too! What this 90-year-old said reminded me of those I spoke with in the military that had made it to the top ranks. I believe 100% of them admitted they wished they had spent more time with their families and loved ones. I too have fell victim to sorrowful reflections in life, but I decided to do something about it and positively affect the future—take good courage! Before I share this next portion from the article, know that the words I previously wrote were from my experience and not this article. I mention that because I'm so surprised to see a great similarity in how I am seeing the world right now several decades from those who are there. Sohn (2019) asked the 90-year-olds what they regretted in life: 1) Not cultivating better relationships with children; 2) Not putting their children on the right path in life; 3) Not taking greater risks to be more loving; 4) Not being better listeners and more empathetic and considerate; 5) Not spending enough time with the people they loved. We can start now and turn these regrets into joy. Please read Sohn's entire article…it was refreshing and thought provoking.

I have concluded that all selfish and greedy human purposes and courses in life lead to nowhere—vanity! Ecclesiastes 1:2-3 reads, "Vanity of vanities, saith the Preacher, vanity of vanities; all is vanity. What profit hath a man of all his labour which he taketh under the sun?" In short, the man or woman focused solely on himself and the cares of this life…end up with nothing at the end of life.

I know where my motto for my house comes from—living from my giving and giving just to live! That's what we do! Growing up on Gearhart Road taught me how to help others and share of your resources to meet the need of the whole. Life has taught me that giving is a one-way act as is love; however, humans have made it two-way. Luke 6:38 exhorts us to "Give, and it shall be given unto you; good measure, pressed down, and shaken together, and running over, shall men give unto your bosom." If you can help others you are Blessed! The amount matters not but it is the willingness to share with others without expectation of something in return.

I discovered my purpose while navigating through life and made many shipwrecks along the way. I can choose to stop and lick my wounds, or I can make the best of the time I have left and fulfill my purpose in life. I must continue to encourage people to pursue their dreams and purpose. Not in vanity, but in community. When God Blesses His people there is always enough and extra to share. I find many people need help escaping negativity and find clasping positivity unnatural. I can recall countless conversations with others about leaving a monetary legacy on earth and my thoughts on this topic changed as I grew older! I pondered on that notion for years and discovered the answer while writing this book. How much money will be enough to last forever? Correct! The legacy is in the deposit we make in the lives of others to help them along the way! The legacy is investing in the generations to follow and warn of pitfalls with conversation and reveal the truth about fame and fortune…hard work precedes. Gearhart Road also taught me hard work is the measure of a man. I am reminded of some of the words of Dr. Martin Luther King, Jr. in his inspiration for "good" hard work and to promote the good for all mankind! Veering off the path is cowardly, but staying the course takes good courage! Numbers 14:24 is a lesson for the courageous who will stay the course, "But my servant Caleb, because he had another spirit with him, and hath followed me fully, him will I bring into the land whereunto he went; and his seed shall possess it!" Joshua and Caleb accompanied the other spies to view the promised land…all their eyes saw the same thing. Listen, because Joshua and Caleb had "another spirit" filled with good courage to conquer whatever was in the way of the promise…notice their seed also had an inheritance or legacy! Parents, one last nugget…your children are watching you! How you handle business, how you handle people, how you handle money, and how you handle challenges! Give your children a fighting chance in this world of challenges—take good courage! I believe in my heart that if you are still reading this manuscript up to this point that you are inspired to go get "it!" Take good courage and possess the land!

The conclusion of the whole matter is found in Ecclesiastes 12:13-14, "Let us hear the conclusion of the whole matter; Fear God and keep his commandments; for this is the whole duty of man. For God shall bring every work into judgment, with every secret thing, whether it be good, or whether it be evil. Dare, to Possess A Good Courage!

BREAKING NEWS…MY EXPERIENCE DURING THE FINAL EDITING PROCESS OF THIS BOOK! MARCH 13, 2022, 0600 HOURS, DAYLIGHT SAVINGS DAY!

To God Be The Glory!

I sewed a miraculous and spontaneous seed of four digits this morning after hearing the Word of God spoken into my life. The man of God on a religious program was a guest speaker the Lord used to speak to me while conscious, I drifted off into a supernatural deep sleep and dream, and God woke me up and I heard Him say "obey the instructions."

In the early morning hours, I was attracted to the choir singing the song He Reigns and that woke me up from a sleep I entered while watching an episode of my lifetime favorite western, Gunsmoke. I have never watched this religious program before in my life, but my faith was activated as the man of God spoke on the power of "wisdom" in my life! The reason I was especially attracted to the message was because it reaffirmed many things I believe and some I have shared in this work.

Wisdom is the principal factor that is tied to all our failures and successes. I listened to the power of the spoken Rhema Word, and it put me in a deeper sleep so real that I thought I was awake.

I heard some critical points that I bear witness in my life, professional, and business experience I share in this book I am praying to release in 2022! I now feel the complete anointing to release this book after enclosing this powerful testimony! The seed is not the harvest, but just the seed I planted to bless 45 million people through this television ministry that will reproduce in 3 ways according to the Word of the Lord I heard, received, and responded to this morning at 0600 hours: 1) Supernatural favor with someone who is able to bless my seed and life abundantly; 2) Supernatural health in a miraculous way; 3) Debt-free home!

I heard the man of God continue to minister as God will bless our business in a supernatural way! Before I heard that Word of the Lord, I was on the phone with the operator to plant my seed, and I was debating which credit card to use and praying fervently because I knew the decision was critical to the seed and harvest! I chose the Success Beyond Boundaries Enterprises (my business) credit card and recalled what was on my heart when I named the company...Blessings and Success...Beyond the Boundaries of my imagination! Then I heard the man of God continue to minister about the harvest that would come to my "business" and life in the next 90 days! Wow...it is just all just making spiritual sense as God is increasing my ability to be a blessing to the world! This is another significant point made in the telecast...what is the "one thing" that you were created to do? We should all know what that is...

The man of God instructed the audience to not call until he finished praying...I received the prayer of faith! When the prayer ended, the thought came to me that the phone might be busy, but I rebuked the thought and was focused on obeying and dialed immediately, and the call went through without delay! I wrote the ending of this book several paragraphs ago... but I was not satisfied until now! I shall include this testimony in the book, but I suspect by the time the book is published I am believing God for a supernatural testimony to bless whoever reads this book of how God used me to bless someone else and experienced the power of God in my life! I have not lost sight of the reason for this seed...to be a blessing to others! I desire my life...to continue to be a river of living waters!

I feel a new anointing even for the ministry that I must continue to release in this world! I'm living from my giving and giving just to live! I was born to encourage and help others and I'm praying at the publishing of this book God continues to use my vessel in His way to bless others in small businesses and all walks of life that I have experienced. I have learned the powerful blessing of asking "questions." A powerful display of humility!

Gems that stood out to me through this experience: Don't be an ignorant Christian...get wisdom; connect with a mentor (coach) and not just friends (cheerleaders); the experiences in my life are a result of the wisdom in my life; things that happen in my life are a result of mistakes (teacher) or wisdom (obedience to God). I thank God for the mentors in my life who told me things I did not want to hear, but I also praise God that I recognized His voice and listened to wisdom from others! I am a teacher still on the hunt for wisdom that I may have wisdom to give. I know I am in the process of God reinventing my life for another dispensation to be a blessing to the world! I'm ready and will let nobody or nothing hinder my faith, my praise, my anointing, or my harvest. Thank you for obedience early this morning...I have not experienced God like this before and it was refreshing to know I am healed, I seek continual forgiveness from those I harmed with unwise acts, I am blessed, as Solomon...I yearn for God's wisdom, I am encouraged in the Lord, and…this is not "the end" but rather, a new beginning!

BREAKING NEWS ONCE AGAIN…I received a supernatural blessing on April 18, 2022! I just had to share the *power* of the Word of God! I am Blessed…to be a Blessing…I'm excited about the next book!

Stay tuned…I am, SBB!

References

AZ Quotes (n.d.). Importance of Education Quotes. Retrieved on February 6, 2021 from https://www.azquotes.com/quotes/topics/importance-of-education.html.

Centers for Disease Control and Prevention (n.d.). Overweight and obesity. Retrieved from https://www.cdc.gov/obesity/data/adult.html on February 18, 2022.

Changing Minds (2018). Values development. Retrieved on August 12, 2018 from http://changingminds.org/explanations/values/values_development.htm.

Cherry, K. (2021). The 5 levels of Maslow's hierarchy of needs. Verywell Mind. Retrieved on October 3, 2021 from The 5 Levels of Maslow's Hierarchy of Needs (verywellmind.com)

Congressional Medal of Honor Society (n.d.). Stories of Sacrifice. Retrieved on November 25, 2020 from https://www.cmohs.org/recipients/john-l-levitow.

Inspiring Behavior (2018). *Physician Leadership Journal, 5*(1), 14.

Merriam-Webster (2020). Dictionary. Retrieved on November 25, 2020 from https://www.merriam-webster.com/

Novak, J. (2018). The six living generations in America. *Marketing Teacher.* Retrieved on August 12, 2018 from http://www.marketingteacher. com/the-six-living-generations-in-america/.

Romaine, P. S. (2007). Positive parenting: building character in young people. *Positive Parenting: Building Character In Young People*, 1-20.

Sky, M. (2018). Emotional suppression causes serious damage to bodies, minds, and spirits. *InnerSelf.* Retrieved on August 16, 2018 from https://innerself.com/content/personal/happiness-and-self-help/ performance/4858-emotional-suppression.html.

Sohn, L. (2019). CNBC Make It. What do 90 somethings regret most? Here's what I learned about how to live a happy, regret-free life. Retrieved from Advice from 90-year-olds: How to live a happy and regret-free life (cnbc.com) on February 18, 2022.

Spall, B. (2021). The core values of the Air Force. Retrieved on October 3, 2021 from The Core Values of the Air Force (benjaminspall.com).

The Annie E. Casey Foundation (2018). Children in single-parent families by race. Kids Count Data Center. Retrieved on August 13, 2018 from https:// datacenter.kidscount.org/data/tables/107-children-in-single-parent- families-by#detailed/1/any/false/870,573,869,36,868,867,133,38,35, 18/10,11,9,12,1,185,13/432,431.

The NeuroAlchemist (2015). How significant emotional events can empower you. *Therapy & Behavioral Change.* Retrieved on August 12, 2018 from http://neuroalchemist.com/2016/03/03/ significant-emotional-events/.

The Ryrie Study Bible (1978). The Moody Bible Institute. King James Version. Moody Press: Chicago, IL.

Workopolis (2018). How many jobs should you expect to hold in your lifetime? Retrieved on February 6, 2021 from https://careers.workopolis.com/advice/how- many-jobs-should-you-expect-to-hold-in-your-lifetime/

Printed in the United States
by Baker & Taylor Publisher Services